Praying Thieves and the God Who Loves Them No Matter What

Praying Thieves

and the God Who Loves Them No Matter What

Anne Marie Drew

morehouse publishing
HARRISBURG, PENNSYLVANIA

Morehouse Publishing, P.O. Box 1321, Harrisburg, PA 17105

Morehouse Publishing is an imprint of Church Publishing Incorporated.

Cover design by Lee Singer

Page design by Lee Singer

Library of Congress Cataloging-in-Publication Data

Drew, Anne Marie.
Praying thieves and the God who loves them no matter what / Anne Marie Drew.
p. cm.
ISBN-13: 978-0-8192-1956-5 (pbk.)
1. Spiritual life—Christianity. 2. Deadly sins. I. Title.
BV4626.D74 2006
242—dc22
2005022615

Printed in the United States of America

01 02 03 04 05 06 07 08 09 10 11 6 5 4 3 2 1

TO JOEY

Ring the bells that still can ring
Forget your perfect offering
There is a crack, a crack in everything
That's how the light gets in.

Leonard Cohen, *Anthem*

Contents

Acknowledgments

Eileen Johnston read drafts of the first two chapters, offering rhetorical and spiritual suggestions. Her Benedictine hospitality continually afforded me a warm welcome. Her stern admonition to turn off the radio helped me avoid unnecessary detours in this manuscript. She has been a cherished source of knowledge and insight. Mindy Smith has served as gatekeeper, computer whiz, and good companion throughout the writing process. Whether we were gasping at the Tiffany's ad or working on the department budget, her quick wit and good humor helped keep life in perspective. Tom and Lane Heath were great sounding boards for my ideas, during long dinners and magical evenings of watching fireflies from the back deck of their home on the Chesapeake Bay. Allyson Booth shared her personal and literary rendering of Dante's circles of hell, while simultaneously helping me negotiate my lived experiences of those same circles.

My fellow pilgrims on the Shalem Pilgrimage to Iona and Lindisfarne had a profound impact. The members of my small group—Nan, Carole, and Dale—taught me the power of the communion of saints. The sweet grace and wisdom of my pilgrimage roommate, Linda Hammond, made her the best of traveling companions. Daniel Drew, the father of the extraordinary trio, offered answers to any number of my questions, including, "What was the name of that city in Israel . . . ?"

Gary Noble, my shadow chair, read multiple drafts of the book, offering his detailed responses as only a scientist might. Even though he was occasionally halfway around the world, first in Kuwait and then in Baghdad, his probing questions forced me to clarify my thinking. Perhaps one day he will come to believe the green words embroidered on a white handkerchief.

And finally, Joey, the blonde bomber, was a wellspring of ideas and encouragement in the writing of this manuscript. He sent me lyrics and quotations. He challenged my theology and my ideas. He's taught me about everything from George Macdonald's meditations to cooking with a vanilla bean . . . and years ago, in my bleakest hours, he forced me to face the tough questions that led to the idea for this book.

Preface

You've never seen an uglier heap of woven cloth. Made of black chenille, with twisted and broken threads, it is a puckered piece of fabric. The remnant was my first attempt at weaving. I had signed up for weaving classes at the suggestion of my friend Eileen and had anticipated pleasant, serene evenings at the loom.

Instead, weaving for me was too much like math: too many calculations and endless attention to details. I didn't know a warp from a weft. Eileen was a naturally gifted weaver, and I envied her superior skills. Some nights, as I sat at my little rented table loom trying to make one small napkin, I'd want to heave a spool of yarn across the room in frustration. I simply could not weave. I refused to give up, however. I relished the challenge of learning something new, of staring down my ineptitude.

I clung to the words of our weaving instructor, who told the class: "Every mistake you make in weaving can be fixed. Don't ever give up and rip the fabric from the loom. If a thread breaks, you can repair it. If you miscalculate and haven't threaded enough heddles, you can add more. If the color scheme doesn't develop the way you thought it might, you can add another color to the pattern. But what's important is to keep weaving, even if you don't like what you create at first. If you stop, you run the risk of never starting again. You don't want the loom to become still and silent."

To the instructor's advice, Eileen added some of her own. "Look," she told me when I showed her a mistake in one of my weaving projects, "imperfections in handwoven cloth are inevitable. That's how we know the fabric isn't machine-made. You can't stop because you make mistakes. Keep weaving."

So I did. Now a beautiful floor loom sits in my home. Cones of yarn fill the shelves of a nearby bookcase. I can be found, of a winter evening, sitting at the loom, creating cloth from almost nothing, weaving prayers into the fabric. The process has become a magical one for me, as the material takes shape from seemingly thin air. I have learned that my instructor was right. There is a way to fix every broken thread. Every hole in the fabric can be repaired. Every thread of yarn is of a piece, with nothing wasted, and everything put to good use. The key is to keep going and not stop. On my loom, there is always a piece in progress. When one piece of fabric comes off, I immediately start working on the next one.

When I go for a walk later on this evening, I will bundle up in a red scarf. Long, ample, and warm, it is the best thing I've woven thus far. Threaded in its texture is a glimmering yarn that catches the light, making the scarf shine from a certain angle. Although this red scarf looks nothing like the black chenille heap I created years ago, the two projects form one piece in my mind. They remind me to persevere.

So, too, God has reminded me of the need to persevere in prayer. No matter the broken threads or the holes in the fabric of my life, I cannot allow my conversation with God to fall silent and still. The temptation to stop praying can be fierce, as anger wells up in me or my spirit stiffens in pride or my energy dissolves into sloth or my loneliness makes me simultaneously desolate and frenetic. But at such times, I remember that second thief on the way to Calvary—a man who had almost nothing left; a man who had seemingly ruined any chance at redemption; a man whose life was a gnarled, black heap of twisted and broken threads. In his bleakest hour, this thief begged Jesus Christ to remember him. And the Lord responded in love, “Today you will be with me in Paradise” (Luke 23:43). And so, no matter what the years bring, no matter how many times or how badly I stumble, I will keep praying.

Chapter 1
The Prayers of Sloppy Sinners

"Please God, don't make me give him up. Please."

As I lay safely on his chest, nestled softly in his arms, feeling his heartbeat, I prayed to keep him. Not to have to surrender him.

I adored this man. We played Scrabble together; wrote books together; went to Orioles games together. We cooked together; tromped on the moors of England together. Walked the shores of Omaha Beach together.

He was the best friend I have ever had. And even as I write, I miss him.

But I had to let him go.

Because my relationship with him kept me from being who God wants me to be. I clung to him for dear life, even as his presence alienated my children and friends. Even as his presence diminished my ability to reach out to other people. I refused, refused to let him go.

Day after day, I'd ask God for a clear sign of what I should do. I didn't hear God say a word. Finally, this man's mother asked me, "Anne Marie, God doesn't have to write it down on a stone tablet, does he?"

And, of course, she was right. The very stones were crying out that this man was not good for me. Still, I needed him. His energy, his devotion, his passion, his ardor, all felt like drops of rain after an emotionally sterile marriage. I was hungry for affection and companionship, for the simple joy of being around someone who didn't consider me a bother.

And, oh! How this man loved my company. When we were at home reading, we'd sit in the same room just to stay close. Even in our king-size bed, we slept close together throughout the night.

There was no room for God. I didn't care.

Still, I prayed and kept talking to God. I figured God could stand to hear the truth. "This man means more to me than you. More to me than my soul. Help me find a way to keep him."

But I knew all along this man was my Isaac. I had to give him back to God.

And I did.

In some ways, the idea for this book was born of the pain of having to let go of the person who meant more to me than my salvation. It was born of my desire to express the unfailing perseverance of a God who wouldn't let me go, who kept turning my face again and again toward the divine presence, until I could stand on my own and grow toward who I'm called to be.

Perhaps because I'm so keenly aware of the arterial tug of misplaced and disordered affections, I was particularly offended when I heard a Christian talk-show host scoff as he mentioned a couple who "pray before they commit adultery." These people were private counseling clients of his, and they had told him how they asked God to grant them strength to end their affair. Scorn saturated his voice as he described this couple on their knees.

His scorn is understandable, but it is misplaced. It's wrong to mock God by begging forgiveness, then sinning with abandon, but I believe people should keep talking to God even as they persist in sin. This adulterous couple isn't behaving like Rasputin, who used prayer to lure women to his bed in the name of God. They are just a man and a woman, flesh and blood, stumbling, simultaneously acknowledging their weakness, afraid of being estranged from God. Their prayers will help prevent that estrangement.

Don't misunderstand me. God will not be mocked. We can't knowingly and willfully pursue sinful, destructive paths without consequence. But we needn't accept the rhetoric of Gregory the Great, who pronounces with medieval vehemence, "For whoever is exalted with pride, whoever is tortured by the longings of covetousness, whoever is relaxed with the pleasures of lust, whoever is kindled by the burnings of unjust and immoderate anger, what else is he but a testicle of the Anti-Christ?" God's approach is more merciful. God holds up a mirror forcing us to see where we fall short. Our Creator will never impel us to conform to divine will, but God presents us with circumstances that lead us into conformity.

Saint Augustine's life offers me great comfort. He struggled with his own fierce attachments to people, even as he deeply loved God and relied on divine mercy. But I was startled when several people disagreed with me. As we discussed the seven deadly sins at a local book club meeting, one young woman said: "Saint Augustine is a perfect example of a hypocrite. He kept doing what he wanted to do, said he was sorry, then everything was supposed to be fine."

Augustine was not a hypocrite, I argued, but a sinner who had suffered mightily in renouncing his lover and their child. Another woman promptly spoke up: "And what about that poor woman? What about the pain he caused her? Why should he be a saint?"

The heated discussion pinpointed the issue at hand. People will sin, make mistakes, and harm others in the process. But they're not necessarily hypocrites. They're doing what all of us must do: finding their way to God. Our flaws don't make us hypocrites. This same book club turned on David for the very same reason. "How could he be a man of God," one woman demanded, "with everything he did wrong?" But David's story, like Augustine's, is our own. Both of them made mistakes—as we do—but those mistakes don't define them, and our mistakes don't define us.

Our transformation, through God's grace, is rather like running a marathon, one of my military colleagues tells me. "If you stop running," he says, "things freeze up on you. You gotta keep going"—no matter what. "Sometimes when I'm running a marathon, I feel like I just have to stop because there's nothing left in me," he explains. "But I keep going. I do the same thing with God. Sometimes I just say, 'God, I need your help,' and somehow I get to the finish line." We don't know where our finish line is. But even though our time on earth is finite and uncertain, there's no statute of limitations on God's love. People with shattered lives and bruised hearts can take decades to respond to God's grace.

A friend of mine told me that his brother flew to Atlanta on September 11, 2001. When his plane landed and he learned of the terrorist attacks, he sought out a priest right in the airport. After years away from God and family, his life turned back toward the Almighty, seemingly in an instant. But it had been more than an instant, of course. For long years, he'd suffered terribly because of the bad decisions he made. When his family pleaded with him to return to a life of faith, he insisted that he was praying even though he wasn't going to church or leading a particularly godly life. Throughout the years when, to all outward appearances, God had no part in this man's life, God had really been there all along. And when September 11 came, there was an open place for God in this man's life. The terrorist attack was the final prompt toward a God who had never turned him away.

Jesus Christ never turns away sinners. He exhorts us to change our ways. He challenges us to transform ourselves into his reflected glory. But he never tells us to go away. The only way we can stay connected to that vibrant love is to keep praying, keep talking to him. We shouldn't be dissuaded in our efforts by some misguided sense of our unworthiness. If we stop praying, we'll lose our longing for God. Inertia and atrophy effect every area of our existence, and our life in God is no different. The longer we stay away from prayer, the easier it becomes not to talk to God, the easier it becomes to forget that we each carry God within us. Even in the midst of prolonged sin, an acquaintance says, be ready for transformation at any moment: "As soon as you see an opening, get out. Don't revel in what you've been doing wrong. Just get out of it, as soon as you feel the nudging of grace."

Most of us have experienced relationships gone sour. Once we learn the skill of not talking to someone, the task becomes easier, until "way leads on to way," to borrow a line from Robert Frost, and diminishing words lead to cold silences. We've all started fitness routines that fall short when we miss one day at the gym, and then another. Pretty soon apathy sets in. The gym membership becomes dormant, until it simply expires. The same thing can happen with prayer. Skipping a day, and then a week, leads to inactivity in general, until we run the risk of letting the membership expire from our own—not God's—lack of attention.

When our life in God stalls, we can't grow into the fullness of our stature in Jesus Christ. We become less able to acknowledge our inner goodness, which is a reflection of our Creator. One of my grown children once told me, "Mom, you're the mirror in which we all see ourselves." Similarly, God serves as the ultimate mirror for all of us. And if we refuse to look at ourselves in God's mirror until we think our reflection is perfect, we'll never see how precious we are. We must persevere in prayer just as we persevere in physical exercise. Sometimes the people we see at the gym are pudgy and fleshy and out of shape, but no physical trainer will suggest that those human beings shouldn't be in the gym until their bodies are buffed and toned. Just so with our God, who doesn't turn us away when our souls are out of shape.

Even when my own prayers reflect little more than my weak will, I keep talking. As I struggled with the disordered relationship that threatened my soul, I wasn't fooling God or myself. We both knew the relationship had to end. Still, only one prayer came to me: "I can't let him go." The fact that I ultimately did let him go proves that God didn't turn a deaf ear.

Traditionally, one way to approach human imperfection was to label seven sins as deadly: Pride, Anger, Envy, Greed, Gluttony, Sloth, and Lust. Within each of these broad categories, there are varying degrees of wrong behavior. Both murderers and quarrelsome people, for example, struggle with anger. The greed that manifests itself as extreme avarice is the same sin that makes some people accumulate too many material possessions for no good reason. Lust, which can foster an inordinate attachment to sexual activity, can also create a disordered grasping of another's affections. All sin, however, is a failure of love. We actively commit an offense that hurts others or ourselves, or we neglect to perform an act of charity. As we strive to grow in grace and love, we allow the Holy Spirit to dwell fully in us, protecting us against our particular sins.

Most of us do tend to fall victim to a particular sin. When I teach *Macbeth*, I always tell my students that the witches know exactly which fault will damn Macbeth to hell: "oe'rweening ambition." The Foul Sisters don't tempt him with money or women, for those aren't his weaknesses. Rather, they dangle in front of him the throne and start his mind whirring about the possibilities of being king. Soon he and his wife are plotting murder.

In Milton's *Paradise Lost*, Satan appeals to Eve's vanity, for that is her weakness. He flatters her outrageously, and she listens and falls into sin. No matter how we understand the forces of evil, we all know that temptation and sin come to us in very personal ways. Though Oreos and Pepsi hold a certain attraction for me, gluttony isn't the sin that hobbles my walk with God. It's lust—not so much carnality, but a yearning to be attached to another at almost all costs. My inordinate attachments to people lead me to periods of mourning when they're no longer within my reach. The mourning suggests that these people belong not to God, but to me, and that their presence in my life matters more than all else.

The seven sins were labeled deadly because people believed they placed our salvation at risk—a person mired too deeply in sin couldn't hope to get to heaven. Today we're less judgmental, but faithful people still understand that certain activities draw us closer to God and others pull us away. Too much pride or anger fills us with such negative emotions and experiences that it's hard to discover an indwelling God. Conversely, sloth pulls the very air out of our souls until we have little sense of self, almost as if we didn't have enough oxygen. Under the weight of each of these sins, we're equally handicapped in our attempts to recognize the God who cherishes us beyond all measure.

Our pilgrimage here on earth is often hobbled by our fear of emptiness and our subsequent attempts to fill that emptiness in damaging ways. When our own mistakes come crashing down on us, we're often tempted to assume that God has finished with us and left us without second chances. On a Sunday-morning walk last fall, I saw a man with a burden that struck me as a metaphor for this feeling of being crippled by sin. Lugging a length of heavy, rusty chain to the bed of his pickup truck, he looked like Jacob Marley from Dickens's *A Christmas Carol*, carrying in death the chains he had forged in life. That Sunday morning, the rusty chains rested on this man's shoulders, forcing his posture into a strained stoop. I wondered how anyone could walk with a burden that heavy.

I once heard Father Patrick Woods, a Catholic missionary, tell a great family story that suggests the burden of our mistakes may not be as heavy as it appears. One of Woods's Christmas duties was the annual ritual of setting up a little lighted village that was stored high up on the top shelf of a closet. One year, as he pulled the cherished family decoration from its shelf, the village fell to the floor, shattering into countless pieces. Distraught, he fetched a broom and dustpan to sweep up the remnants. His young niece, who had witnessed the disaster, went to get a bottle of glue. When he told her that the damage was too great to be repaired, she insisted that they at least try. Together they pieced the village back together and plugged it in.

The brightness shining forth was greater than ever, as the light streamed through all the broken places.

Perhaps Judas is the classic example of a sinner who believed he was smashed and damaged beyond redemption. When he tried to return the thirty pieces of silver to the chief priests, he said, "I did wrong to deliver up an innocent man!" They retorted: "What is that to us? It is your affair" (Matt 27:3–4). Judas didn't have a niece to tell him to pick up the broken pieces. In his despair, he turned to people who had no interest in bearing him up. We can't, at this distance, know what prompted Judas to betray Jesus. But whether greed or jealousy or anger motivated him, he turned his back on God. And having turned away, he never found the faith to face God again. Yet there can be no doubt that Jesus himself forgave Judas. There is not one example to indicate otherwise. Not one. No matter the harm done, no matter the degree of sin, Jesus loves and forgives. God does the transforming. We simply allow the Creator to work in us.

Andrew Solomon, in his book *The Noonday Demon: An Atlas of Depression*, talks about the need to "mobilize love" during severe bouts of depression.[1] What is true of depression is also true of all of life's ills, for when we feel guilty or unworthy, we, like Judas, isolate ourselves from others and from God. The isolation starts to wear us down. It reinforces our sense that we're unworthy and fall short of our goals. Like Doubting Thomas, who needed the flesh-and-blood reassurance of a resurrected love, we too need something tangible to help us through the rough spots in life. The grace of other people often carries the grace of God. Counselors sometimes recommend that despondent people carry with them at all times an index card listing the names and phone numbers of people who love them, who can be called at times of distress. Simply carrying such a card can diminish the sometimes lethal sense of unworthiness. There might be wisdom in writing the name of God at the top of the card. Though such a practice might smack of sentimentality, we sometimes need the most elementary reminders that God is with us.

Every single one of my dearest friends, like me, has serious flaws that they wrestle with and try to overcome. On certain days, these flaws seem to be smeared over every good thing. The holiest, most prayerful person in my universe steadily struggles against her particular weakness, yet she will rouse herself from sleep to pray with me in my bleakest, most desperate hours. Once, at midnight, she called to say she'd been awakened with an immediate sense of my need for prayer. So she prayed, "Lord, send your angels to Annie's house. Right now, Lord. Do not delay. Place a guard in every room, and make your angels lift her up. Hold her until she feels your love."

I felt as if the grace of God poured into my home and that I was a well-loved friend and child of the Creator. Once I called this same friend from Lucerne, Switzerland, when I'd had a spiritual breakthrough. It was two o'clock in the morning in Lucerne and I had no idea if she'd be home, but when she answered the phone, it seemed as if the divine presence scurried back and forth across the Atlantic as we prayed. I was halfway around the world, but when we prayed, we were drawn closer to the heart of God. God has never said to the two of us: "Oh you two again. You two have used up all the coupons. Mend your flaws and then we'll talk." The Lord of all life surrounds us at every turn, reminding us that our true identity flows from who we are before God.

Thomas à Kempis's *Imitation of Christ* first drove home the notion, for me, that my identity before God defines me. No matter what my worst enemies or my beloved friends may think, I must be mindful of who I am before God. God has never said a bad thing about me. When I place myself in God's presence and say, "Who am I?" God never says, "You are a willful, self-centered woman, catapulted around by her emotions, prone to anger and lustful thoughts." Even when I've dragged myself in tears to a prayer chapel, God has never condemned me. God just is. God loves. Certainly God challenges and beckons. But God does not condemn.

I can't count all the ways God has sustained me. One particularly rough March, right after I'd been divorced, while the pain was still so raw that I had trouble getting out of bed in the morning, my son Tony came to visit. After he left, I had some errands to run, and on the windshield of my car I found a note he'd left me scribbled on a napkin, the only piece of paper he could find. On the napkin, he'd written "MOM" and encircled the word in a heart. He had also written, "Life will be great from this moment on!!" The napkin from that long-ago March is in my Bible. On the windshield or in my Bible, the napkin reminds me not only of my beloved son, but also of the piercing goodness of life and of a God who never stops loving us. As we are reminded in Matthew, "So it is not the will of your Father in heaven that one of these little ones should be lost" (18:14).

Saint Mary's Church here in Annapolis has a perpetual adoration chapel, a place open for prayer twenty-four hours a day. I have sometimes practically crawled into that chapel, in the throes of great sin and even greater sorrow. Sometimes mustering only a simple prayer, "Here I am Lord," I sit there, lumplike, convinced that I'm wasting God's time. But of course, I'm not.

During one chapel visit, when my leaden despair overpowered me, I quietly turned to the two people sitting nearby reading their Bibles and asked: "Could you please pray for me? I'm in bad shape." Without a word, they both got on their knees and prayed. Neither of them said to me, "I am busy with my own prayers; please do not disturb me." Without hesitation, without pause, they prayed for me, a woman they didn't know. As each of them left the chapel that day, they patted me on the shoulder. They were God's agents that day, reminding me that I'm not alone, not forsaken.

What confuses us during great sin is that we know how badly botched our lives are. We've hurt other people. We've hurt ourselves. We've compromised our own integrity, perhaps our reputations. Like Judas, we truly believe our wrongdoing can't be redeemed.

I have an old, unwearable bathrobe that's come to symbolize my darkest hours, hours when a gnarled mass of emotions and fury seemed to define me. One night that seemed particularly God-forsaken burns in my memory. Angry and violent recriminations had filled my home all evening, and the legions of hell seemed unleashed all around me. Alone and miserable, I was keenly aware of the mess I'd created. My PhD, my great job, my publications, my cherished children, my glorious friends—nothing mattered. There I was, a mass of human sorrow, wrapped in a terrycloth bathrobe, my tears simultaneously filling my throat and drenching my cheeks. Everything good seemed beyond my reach. There was to be no redemption that night. I sobbed myself to sleep, sustained by nothing more than the sheer force of will that made me stay alive.

There have been stretches of such nights in my life when the effort to draw breath felt pointless, when life seemed an impossibly long and arduous burden. During those bleak periods, I tended to agree with those people who founded the Ephrata Cloister in Lancaster County, Pennsylvania, who believed that life was simply a vale of tears to be endured. At such times, the knowledge that God loved me didn't matter at all. I didn't care. But somehow, through the sheer, overpowering force of grace, I survived.

Some of my worst bleak stretches came attached to a great love in my life. I still, even at this distance, can't pretend to understand the implications of everything that happened, but I do know that I adored this man beyond all imagining. My experience with this man confirmed what I know to be true. Each of us is a study in contrasts. One day, one moment, we are our best selves; the next minute, our bleaker side emerges.

In William Shakespeare's *Hamlet*, King Claudius faces a spiritual mess. His manifold and brutal sins force him to his knees in prayer, but he's not ready to make amends for his sins, so he states, "Pray can I not." But he keeps trying and in agony cries out, "Help, angels." Claudius doesn't deserve too much sympathy, but he's entitled to his prayer. At least he persists in staying in touch with heaven. Macbeth, on the other hand, decides after a few murders that he's steeped so deeply in blood that turning around is more trouble than continuing in sin. Like Judas, he decides he's past forgiveness and commits the ultimate sin of despair.

That despair can manifest itself in many ways. For example, after the temporary increase in church attendance following September 11, 2001, I heard a wag say: "Sure, people went back to church. But they only went long enough to remember why they stopped going in the first place." And one of those reasons might well be the sense that sinners are unwelcome. That even Jesus doesn't want us in the pews. That if we have a grievance against a brother, we have to fix the grievance first and then come back. But when Jesus tells us not to be like whited sepulchers, he is telling us to *try* to make amends before we go to church. We can't just complain and moan about our grievances and then go to church. Church is, after all, a hospital for sinners. We may have unresolved differences with others, we may have flaws in need of mending, but we belong in the communion of saints, nonetheless.

Thus the message of the Gospels is that we must keep talking to God, even when we know we're sinning. Of course, there is a contradiction here—some might even say blasphemy. But I'd argue that we all want to be like the second thief on Calvary. Painfully aware of our own sinfulness, we still talk to the Savior. Whether we need healing or confession, we need to turn to God. Our sins can grow from a lack of self-worth or they can fester because of obdurate pride and willfulness, but our spiritual task remains the same: Keep praying, keep lifting our minds and hearts to God, so that God can help us discover our true path.

The story of the two thieves in Luke's gospel never loses its grip on my imagination. We don't know if the thieves were wounded by the hurts their lives had inflicted on them—or if they were just plain obstinate. Perhaps, like most of us, they were a combination of both. Three of the gospel writers mention the thieves only as being a taunting presence at Golgotha. According to Matthew, "Two insurgents were crucified with him, one at his right and one at his left" (27:38). Mark writes, "With him they crucified two insurgents, one at his right and one at his left . . . [they] likewise kept taunting him" (16:27, 32). And John says, "There they crucified him, and two others with him: one on either side" (19:18).

Luke gives more details: "Two others who were criminals were led along with him to be crucified. When they came to Skull Place, as it was called, they crucified him there and the criminals as well, one on his right and one on his left. One of the criminals hanging in crucifixion blasphemed him: 'Aren't you the Messiah? Then save yourself and us.' But the other one rebuked him: 'Have you no fear of God, seeing you are under the same sentence? We deserve it, after all. We are only paying the price for what we've done, but this man has done nothing wrong.' He then said, 'Jesus, remember me when you enter upon your reign.' And Jesus replied, 'I assure you; this day you will be with me in paradise'"(Luke 23:43).

The story of the two thieves is justifiably understood as one of redemption, but I am far more interested in one detail that Luke offers and the other gospel writers do not: that the two thieves walked along with Jesus on the way to Golgotha. They weren't already there, and they didn't just appear. They struggled with him, carrying their own burdens. And the second thief, all along the painful, desperate path of the Via Dolorosa, must have been thinking about his life and what he'd done, the accumulated wrongdoings. One wonders whether he kept his eyes on Jesus when the Savior fell. Whether he watched as Jesus comforted the daughters of Jerusalem. Something about Jesus softened his heart. In those last few moments of his earthly existence, he turned toward God, while the other thief turned away. Somewhere in the walk, in the suffering, on the way to Golgotha, one of the thieves responded and became who God had intended him to be all along. The apparent end was the starting point for this man, further proof that we can turn to God no matter where we are on our journey.

Our own world, our own small circles contain many people who struggle as mightily as the second thief. I think of a young friend of mine who recently suffered a harsh professional loss at the hands of an unfair boss. She acknowledges that God is asking her to let go of her rage and bitterness, but of those fierce emotions she says, "Please, I want to hang onto them for a little while longer." She knows that no matter how she's been wronged, she has to forgive. But for now, the comfort of her negative emotions is stronger than her ability to turn those emotions over to God. This young woman loves God, talks to her Creator daily, prays for the strength to survive her public loss and humiliation—but she will not, just now, forego her anger. A head basketball coach whose identity had been wrapped up in her ability to teach basketball, she had her program stripped from her for reasons that aren't yet clear. She is trying mightily to resurrect her life. But for now, she wants to be angry, to hate the athletic director. She knows that Jesus would have her let go of these feelings, but for now, her flesh and blood cannot yield.

Then there's me, the sloppiest of sinners, who, after gathering the strength to end the grief-strewn relationship, still tried to fill my bed with stuff so as not to notice the emptiness. For months, I slept on one small part of a king-size bed. The other three-quarters were covered with my Bible, a script for a play I was directing, the TV remote, a *Good Housekeeping* magazine, a volume of Shakespeare, and, at night, my two cats, Charlie and Henry. All those things on the bed helped fill the space I experienced as empty.

Sometimes at night I'd remember a conversation I had with my father when I was in the throes of my difficulties. He asked me, "How can you keep going to church if you're shacking up with some guy?"

"If I stop talking to God now," I replied, "I may never find my way back."

In all my confusion and misery and sense of unworthiness, I did keep talking. And God never once told me to go away, never asked the question my father did. God never said, "Get your act cleaned up, then I'll listen." God listened all along and finally showed me the way out. Prayer helped me stay open, more aware of God's presence and grace.

God uses a variety of means to show us the way out of our own blindness and to draw us to our Creator in love. A young lieutenant in my department at the Naval Academy, where I teach English, now a man of deep faith, was for years quite proud of his atheism. Refusing to make a distinction between Christianity and flawed Christians, he prided himself on "seeing through the facade of organized religion." He was fascinated by matters of faith but steadfastly resisted believing in God. One spring evening, he attended a live performance of Mozart's *Requiem* at the Academy. After the performance, he took a walk in the clear night air with the stars shining and said, "I believe." He accepted the Incarnation as real. Seemingly in a moment, God pierced through his pride and claimed him. He wasn't overlooked because of his pride. The flaw didn't matter to God. The human being did.

When we read of Moses or Paul or any of the great saints, it's easy to assume their lives were different from ours—that they knew, on a fundamental level, where they were headed. They knew for sure what God wanted of them, and therefore their sacrifices, their faith journeys were not as painful as ours. Even their worst sins seem to us tidy, contained. In his book *Walking the Bible*, Bruce Feiler offers a more realistic view of such people when he describes them as human beings "going forth from a world they knew to a world that didn't yet exist based solely on the word of a god they'd never actually seen."[2] The terror, the anger, the recriminations, the sin, if you will, of their lives pulsed through their journey of faith.

Our faith starts to waiver in those stretches of sin when we falter and turn our backs on God, when we turn away from love. We start to question whether any eternal reward can be worth sacrificing our temporal comforts. And because sin makes us self-centered, we can no longer discern correctly. We become so convinced of our own unworthiness or inflated with our own pride that we hinder not only our own spiritual paths, but the paths of others as well. When our own arteries are clogged with spiritual debris, we are less able to advance the Kingdom of God here on earth. We are handicapped in our attempts to know, love, and serve God.

The way out of sin isn't tidy. Sanctification is a sloppy process. Often we're held by something we know is wrong. A demon that holds us so tightly that it doesn't even feel like a demon anymore. It just feels like life.

But always there is Jesus Christ, who even on his way to Calvary, bearing the unbearable load of grief and suffering, could emanate enough grace to catch hold of the second thief and draw him to heaven. God draws us to heaven, against our will sometimes, never, ever closing the door in our faces.

One night, when my whole life felt like one closed door, I snuggled into the chair in my prayer corner and started to read the Gospel of Matthew, straight through. I'm not sure what I expected to find, but I was searching for some solace for my sense of isolation. Matthew seemed like he might be good company. Before long, I grabbed a paper and pencil and started taking notes. The rush of the love story was overwhelming. And it is a love lived out in the middle of the noisiest, sloppiest lives. Matthew's Gospel is not tidy. Rather, it is decidedly untidy.

Disorder can be comforting to sinners like me. As I reread Matthew's Gospel, I remembered standing on the shores of the Mediterranean, feeling very close to God, near that raging, dark, and stormy sea. I thought of Jesus living out his life in that region, a world where, as a friend of mine says, "one conversation can erupt into five." Matthew's love story is set against such turbulence. The people in the Gospel are smelly, testy, irrational, lustful, greedy, pompous, ridiculous—and Jesus Christ loves them, again and again. Without ceasing. He understands that they are flawed; he exhorts them to be their best selves; but he never, ever stops loving them.

In my rereading of Matthew, I stopped counting how many demons were cast out, how many cures effected. The sheer volume of the cures indicates Jesus' tireless efforts on behalf of suffering people.

And what a group of people they were. A leper. A paralyzed boy. Peter's mother-in-law. A demoniac. A ragtag group of flawed and miserable souls, touched by the hand of God. There's no guarantee that these people, once cured, were secure for life. Certainly, in the subsequent years and decades of their lives, their faith might have weakened. Their momentary encounter with Jesus, though piercing and life changing, was only momentary. They had to go on with their lives, as do we—buoyed up by the lived knowledge of a loving God, but sometimes floundering as we lose sight of that same God.

We're all part of the ragtag group that God surrounds with transforming love.

In John Irving's novel *A Prayer for Owen Meany*, Owen is a young boy who routinely offers spiritual insight, insisting that God loves us no matter how many mistakes we make. He is a Christlike character who "speaks" in all capital letters. Linking our failings to those of the disciples, Owen says: "IT'S TRUE THAT THE DISCIPLES ARE STUPID—THEY NEVER UNDERSTAND WHAT JESUS MEANS, THEY'RE A BUNCH OF BUNGLERS. THEY DON'T BELIEVE IN GOD AS MUCH AS THEY *WANT* TO BELIEVE, AND THEY EVEN BETRAY JESUS. THE POINT IS, GOD DOESN'T LOVE US BECAUSE WE'RE SMART OR BECAUSE WE'RE GOOD. WE'RE STUPID AND WE'RE BAD AND GOD LOVES US ANYWAY."[3]

God does love us anyway, even when our lives aren't testimonies of simple grace and stunning redemption. Some of us drag ourselves kicking and screaming through the mud to face a God we're not even so sure we want to spend time with. But always, like the still small voice that captured Elijah or the Hound of Heaven who captured Francis Thomson, we're pursued by a God who won't let us go. We're pursued by a lavish God who at the wedding feast of Cana filled more than a hundred jugs with wine. No one was sipping wine at the feast. The wine flowed freely and abundantly. That lavish God stands by us as we sin, listening when all we can offer is the sorry confusion and mess that we've created.

PRAYER SUGGESTIONS

An Encounter with Jesus

Read Chapters 8 and 9 of Matthew's Gospel, straight through. As you read, keep your eye on Jesus Christ and his interaction with a wide range of wounded and flawed people.

If you were to add your own story to Matthew's Gospel, what might you tell Jesus? Might you tell him about an addiction? A troubled relationship? An illness? An obsession? If you knew you had the undivided attention of Jesus Christ, what might you say to him?

Take some time and imagine what this gracious and merciful man might say to you in return.

You Are Beloved

Read Matthew 3:13–17. Read it again. Then substitute your name for the word *son*, and repeat the phrase aloud. For example, "This is my beloved, Elizabeth, in whom I am well pleased." When the weight of your own limitations presses down heavily, you might call this sentence to mind, reminding yourself that the Lord says of each of us what is said of Jesus: *You are beloved.*

Chapter 2
Praying with an Angry Heart

A former colleague recounts an almost unbelievable story that he's painfully labeled "The Box in the Attic," a story that chronicles his wife's years of betrayal. Rummaging around in the attic one day looking for a box of Thanksgiving decorations, he came across an old plastic milk crate. Neatly arranged inside the red plastic container was a series of manila folders, labeled in his wife's hand. The tabs were all calligraphically inscribed with the first names of men. With his heart twisting, he pulled one folder from the crate and began reading. He found himself reading love letters, written to his wife from a series of men, since the beginning of their marriage. With nearly self-destructive speed, as he tells it, he tore through the other folders, reading cards and little love notes and seeing snapshots of his wife and these men. Scribbled on top of one particularly long letter were these words: "Maybe you better burn this after you read it so that *you know who* doesn't see it." This man actually vomited right there on the attic floor. Then he slowly gathered up several folders and descended the attic stairs. When he glimpsed his wife sitting at the kitchen table drinking coffee, he had a momentary impulse to rip the cup from her hand and throw the steaming hot beverage in her face.

This couple is no longer married. The pattern of betrayal and deceit evidenced in the letters was too lethal. My colleague had felt that his wife, a professional who traveled quite a bit, had been turning her affections away from him. The letters proved him right. He has since told me that he was driven almost to the point of violence: "With my bare hands, I could have strangled the life out of her. I wanted to smash her face into the kitchen table and pound it again and again until she was just sheer pulp. My guardian angels must have saved me."

Anger can range from the minor irritations that rise up every day to an overwhelming feeling of uncontrollable rage. Simple displeasure over another's actions can cause us to respond in bitter, hardened ways. We come to pit ourselves against the rest of the world, becoming incapable of either dispensing or accepting the love of God. Too busy being indignant and hostile, we can fail miserably in any attempt to live with fairness and justness. In writing of his own struggles with anger, poet W. H. Auden mentioned that his British upbringing "strongly discouraged overt physical expressions of anger," so that at his most vehement, all he ever did was slam a door. He did mention, however, that he grew angry if he was dealt a poor hand at cards, if he waited at a long red light, or if he couldn't get a seat in a crowded restaurant.[1] Anyone striving to live fully in the Spirit knows that all of those leanings toward anger need to be examined and turned over to God. Few of us, certainly, will become so angry that we'll commit murder, but we've probably been mad enough to snap at an ineffective store clerk or hang up the phone in a huff.

Most of us probably have a litany of angry responses: We'll denigrate a coworker or family member. We'll utter nasty epithets at someone who cuts us off in traffic. When our strong sense of self pits us against others, we fail to see others as human beings whom God loves. Anger, whether we slam doors or seethe inwardly, can hinder our growth in grace. Prayer can move us away from anger and toward tenderness.

Unlike Auden, I have known murderous rage, far closer to what my colleague experienced after his discovery of the box in the attic. I hope never again to be poisoned by the venom that wracked my most life-wounding moments, moments when my prayers were simply inarticulate pleas for hope and reassurance. I'm grateful that the Lord of the universe heard and sustained me.

Knowing full well that I alone am responsible for my rage, I'm no longer tempted to lay blame at another's doorstep. I've come to understand that the rage was a way of fending off a perceived void in my existence. By filling myself with fury, I was trying to harden myself against further pain. Still, the multiple hurts and cruelty aimed at me gave me ample reason to become enraged. For more than twenty years, I was married to a minister who placed his church above his family. A self-acknowledged workaholic, he now understands how misplaced his affections and energies sometimes were. As a fledgling minister with a young family, however, his need to be valued in his pastoral role was more important to him than his roles as husband and father. As I felt increasingly ignored and abandoned, my hurt turned into rage, and the marriage developed into a volatile pattern of seething grief.

My vocal complaints about my husband's inordinate attachment to his job made some of his parishioners feel very sorry for him. Some female parishioners were particularly sympathetic. Early in the marriage, a woman tugged me by the arm one day as I was loading my baby daughter into my Volkswagen bug. Securing six-month-old Francesca in her car seat, I turned to see what this woman wanted. She looked me dead in the eyes and announced, "You will never understand your husband the way I do." Now, the fact that she was probably right didn't take away the sting of her words. Another woman said, "When are you going to abandon your stubborn will and realize that the church is more important than you and your kids?"

As this vicious cycle wound tighter and tighter, my ability to be objective all but disappeared. Whenever I'd walk into my husband's office and see yet another statue or cross-stitched sampler from a female parishioner, I felt diminished. Whenever a troubled woman in the middle of a divorce came to my husband seeking counseling, I grew worried. When I answered the phone at six in the morning and then again at midnight to hear a sobbing woman say, "Please, I just need to talk to him," my heart turned over in my chest. When, on Valentine's Day, grateful women gave him cheery little cards affirming their affection for him, I became distraught.

We had three small children, all under the age of four. The difficult birth of our second son had left me physically weakened and emotionally drained. I needed and wanted a husband who valued me, to whom I mattered more than anything but God. I didn't have such a spouse.

My husband's adamant refusal to alter his work schedule combined with my volatile emotions to fuel the incendiary situation. His stubbornness inflamed my anger. I'd throw things. I'd scream. I once overheard the little boy next door saying of me, "She's always yelling." He was right. I was furious. It was all of a piece; I was being minimized to invisibility while my husband was emotionally uninvested.

One evening at about five o'clock, when my husband called to say he wouldn't be home for dinner because one of his female parishioners was in a crisis, I lost control. The woman in question had made him late for dinner at least eight times in the previous month. There I was with meatloaf, macaroni and cheese, applesauce, and three small kids—but I was straight-armed yet again by my husband's need to put the church first. Enraged, I hung up the phone just as poor Joey, my two-year-old, walked into the kitchen and accidentally spilled a carton of milk all over the kitchen floor. I exploded. I yanked that little boy by the hair, by his beautiful, cornsilk curls, and shook him fiercely. When I was done, there in my hand was a tuft of his soft, blond hair. No matter how many times

I've revisited that moment, my heart shrinks inside me from the memory of his hair in my hands.

When I told my dad about that incident, I said: "These people are being horrible. I know Joey didn't deserve what I did, but I'm so mad. These women are invading our home, and my husband's not doing anything to stop it."

My wise father gave me some of the sagest advice I've ever received: "Sweetie," he said, "no matter what anyone is doing to you, you are responsible for how you behave. Anyone can be decent when people treat them well. The true test of character comes in how you treat those who are cruel to you. You keep up this anger and rage, and you'll be a bitter woman before long. And when people meet you decades from now, all they'll see is the hardened person you've become. They won't know or care how you got to be that way. All they'll know is that you are a hard and brittle shrew."

My father was right. I was in a situation that left me feeling enraged all the time, and I needed to determine what to do. God doesn't ask anyone to live with abuse, nor does God demand that we act as doormats for those who treat us poorly. Although my relationship with my husband was deeply flawed, I was determined to find the good in my marriage and, in so doing, the strength to keep the family together. My three glorious children were ample reason. In addition, I liked being married to a man who understood the importance of God in both my life and his own. So there was enough good to make me persevere. But even so, there was neglect and lack of concern for my welfare and that of our children, and it was real and harmful. Despite my best efforts to put a good face on it, my rage at the injustice grew exponentially. I really knew how my colleague felt after finding that box in the attic.

Is it too horrible for me, a middle-aged English professor, to admit that years ago as a wife and mother, my jealousy and rage drove me to do ungodly things and think nearly unspeakable thoughts—only the smallest hint of which is recorded here?

At times, I see myself in Rosa Dartle, from Charles Dickens's *David Copperfield.* She is consumed with murderous jealousy when she discovers that Steerforth, the man she has loved since childhood, has run off with another woman. Rosa lashes out in anger at the young woman who has seemingly stolen the man she loves. "I would have her branded on the face, dressed in rags, and cast out in the streets to starve," she declares. "If I had the power to sit in judgment on her, I would see it done. See it done? I would do it! I detest her. If I ever could reproach her with her infamous condition, I would go anywhere to do so. If I could hunt her to her grave, I would. If there was any word of comfort that would be a solace to her in her dying hour, and only I possessed it, I wouldn't part with it for Life itself."[2]

In those early years of my marriage, I was Rosa Dartle angry. Suffice it to say that when I teach this scene in my classes, I have no trouble understanding the words. Even now, rather than following my usual practice of allowing students to read passages aloud in class, I reserve this one for myself. Although her words are horrible and hateful, they continue to be a cathartic release for me.

Always, in those early, dreadful years of my marriage, God kept nudging me, and I prayed, "God, grant me a heart strong enough to endure the struggle." God granted my prayer. Had I totally stopped praying through those years, I probably would have turned into the bitter shrew my father warned of. I would have become Rosa Dartle. I relied often in those years on the Jesus Prayer, the simple repetition of the words, "Lord Jesus, Son of God, have mercy on me a sinner." Some days, I couldn't even muster the strength to recite the whole sentence. I'd say shorter and shorter versions of the plea for help, until I'd simply say one word, "Lord," as a way of breaking the momentum of chaos and fear.

In the finished attic of this very angry house, I had a prayer corner, barely big enough for a table and rug. Often, late at night, I simply sat in this corner of the house, where no battle had ever been waged, no harm had ever been done to anyone. Seeking God's presence, I'd read the Psalms and Isaiah and let myself be reassured that God was right there next to me. Beyond the reassurance of the divine presence, I wanted to be reassured that there was hope, that even in the midst of the chaotic turmoil that seemed to be all around, there was light and grace. Isaiah 55:1, with its invitation to grace, filled me with great hope:

> "You who have no money,
> come, receive grain and eat;
> Come without paying and without cost,
> drink wine and milk."

In those days, when I had nothing to barter with, no currency to offer God, only my brokenness, I wrapped myself in Isaiah's insistence that we are indeed loved and cherished, no matter what our state.

I also gained great strength, then and now, from the narrative of Corrie Ten Boom's family's life in a concentration camp during the Holocaust. Amid unimaginable inhumanity, she and her sister found ways to pray and stay hopeful and kind. Years later, when delivering a speech, she spotted one of her former Nazi guards in the audience and didn't know how to muster the grace to extend her hand to him in greeting. She describes the feeling that God guided her hand into the extended hand of her former torturer, as the guard reached out to her. God helped her do what she lacked the strength to do herself.

It can never be said enough: God is a God of miracles. The infinite power of grace will surprise and redeem at every turn. When, at my mother-in-law's funeral, I was greeted by one of my husband's hurtful parishioners, God immediately brought the Corrie example to mind, enabling me to extend my hand in greeting. My handshake was perfunctory and curt, and I couldn't manage to act with the full grace of Corrie Ten Boom, but I believe I did what God gave me the grace to do. My attempt to be gracious, even with a still-hurting heart, made me think of a retreat director's remark: "God meets us where we are." Our Creator is active, continually offering us grace and protecting us until we can act with a heart full of love. God helped me extend my hand to that former parishioner. Maybe the next time I face her, my heart will be more like God's.

God's mercy extends to all of us, however, even when we can't or don't control our rage. I learned this lesson from a prison chaplain years ago. During my freshman year at college, I volunteered to attend a prison Christmas worship service. The organizing group of volunteers didn't want the prisoners to feel alone during the holiday. I will never forget the stunning words of the chaplain's sermon. Looking out at the group of hardened and bitter prisoners—men who'd killed, maimed, and raped other human beings—the chaplain said: "God wants you to be happy. No matter what you've done, no matter if you're here in jail, God is right here with you and wants to give you peace and calm. On this Christmas morning, remember how valuable you are to God. No matter what crimes you have committed." Sitting on that worn wooden pew in that prison chapel, with its dirty yellow walls, smell of stale cigarette smoke, and frayed hymnals, I realized that no matter what these men had done—and their crimes were atrocious and violent ones—they were being held in the palm of God's hand. I was overwhelmed with a sense of God's presence, even in the midst of the collective misery of these men and their victims. I've often wondered through the years about those prisoners and the effect of that Christmas morning sermon on them. I know its effect on me. Those words from that long-ago Christmas morning have sustained me, especially in the midst of my own transgressions, when I, like those prisoners, was trapped in fury and rage.

One of my friends runs a safe haven, a place where she takes in all kinds of people in need. Her experience has helped me understand how many people struggle with the effects of anger. Over the years, she's sheltered a score of battered and abused women. They often return to their husbands, desperately believing that, like Saul of Tarsus, their spouses will have a Damascus road experience and be transformed. My friend prays with these women as they take the necessary steps to break the cycle of abuse. They know that God doesn't want them to stay in deadly situations—situations that frequently cause their own violent tendencies to surface. But often they can't garner enough strength to establish independent lives. With my friend, they pray until God shows them an alternate path and they find the courage to take it.

My students have described frightening fights with their boyfriends or girlfriends. One young woman told me about a fight she'd had with her boyfriend the previous night, "I just knew if I didn't hit something, my chest was going to explode," she told me. So she punched the wall. She was discouraged and stunned by her own behavior. A person of faith, she wanted reassurance and hope. "Women aren't supposed to get that mad, are they?" she asked me as she sat in my office. "Only guys are, right?" She clearly wanted to talk about the issue, so I told her about teaching William Golding's *Lord of the Flies* to a group of high school girls. It's about a group of boys stranded on a desert island who turn into a pack of savages, unleashing horrible violence and eventually killing each other. The book conveys brilliantly the depravity of which we're all capable, given the right circumstances.

These long-ago female high school students absolutely missed the point of the novel. When we had finished the book, and I was feeling confident the high schoolers had understood the message, I asked, hypothetically, "How might this story have been different if it had been a bunch of girls stranded on the island rather than boys?"

One girl piped up, "Oh! With girls, none of the violence ever would have happened. Girls would have taken care of each other and been very maternal—not violent." Her classmates nodded in agreement, seemingly unaware that even a group of women can behave savagely.

This story caused the young woman sitting in my office to chuckle. "They sure had a lot to learn, didn't they?"

The tricky thing about anger is that sometimes its worst effects aren't visible. The quiet hardening of the heart that occurs can be so insidious. The Bible admonishes us, "If today you hear his voice, harden not your hearts." That's vital, because if we don't listen today, we may not hear tomorrow. God won't stop talking. We'll simply forget the sound of God's voice. We'll forget where to look or how to listen. One of my friends, whose husband is currently deployed in the Persian Gulf, sometimes calls his office phone here in the States late at night, merely to hear the recorded sound of his voice message. Because he's in the middle of the desert, her chances of talking to him in real time are almost nonexistent. Still, she longs for the sound of her beloved's voice. One of my former professors, a widower, was so grateful to have his children around him, living reminders of the wife he cherished. "I hear her voice when they talk," he tells me. Like Elijah, who catches the sound of God's voice on the wind, we have to stay attuned.

One prayer technique that has helped me move past intense grief and rage, the resulting sense of unworthiness, and the potential for a hardened heart comes from David Hassel's book *Radical Prayer*—in particular, what Hassel calls "Prayer of Personal Reminiscence."[3] As we gently and quietly call to mind a painful incident from the past, we can place Jesus in the scene in our mind's eye, focusing on Christ's presence in the incident. I have found this kind of prayer to be extraordinarily effective, and the Prayer Suggestions at the end of this chapter illustrate how you can use this method to pray over an angry incident.

This prayer practice bears stunning results, because God always turns up right where you least expect. When I used this prayer to review the sorrowful incident of pulling poor Joey's hair,

I discovered that Jesus Christ was standing right there in that kitchen, watching with a look of such anguish and love on his face. He wasn't doing anything. He was just there.

I've have come to understand that the fact of God's just being there is a supreme anchor, a solid mainstay. There is absolutely no place where God is not, and there is no person with whom God does not dwell. Over the years, the thought of God's omnipresence has been a source of true comfort for me. Practicing the Prayer of Personal Reminiscence makes graphically clear how immediate is the divine presence. I once read a book about relationships in which the male author wanted women to understand that they'd always want to spend more time with their mates than their mates wanted to spend with them—it's just a difference between the genders and must be accepted as fact, he argued. Reading this made me think of how God never gets enough of us and never says to us: "I've already spent two hours listening to you. I'm busy now." Even in the midst of our deepest anguish, deepest anger, God is closer than our next thought.

In praying over the incidents in the New Testament where Jesus is moved to anger, I've come to understand that anger, in and of itself, isn't wrong. Jesus did indeed get angry—very angry—but he never lashed out in manic rage. When Jesus chased the money changers from the temple, he "fashioned a whip out of cords" (John 2:15). In meditating on the scene, I kept asking myself why he would take the time, in a moment of rage, to make a weapon. In some ways, the action makes him seem intent on inflicting severe physical punishment. As I puzzled over the incident, I grew more confused. A friend of mine, a scientist who has a reason for everything, has a theory: "I think he was giving himself time to channel the anger and get it under control. He didn't want to lash out in a blind rage. He wasn't seeking hand-to-hand combat. He was slowing himself down."

A similar incident occurs when the woman caught in adultery is dragged before the Lord, fresh from bed, with crowds clamoring for her death. In the midst of the hysteria, Jesus stops and draws in the sand. We may never know what he was drawing in the sand, but a colleague surmises: "He was thinking about what he was going to say. He was thinking."

Perhaps my friend is right. The Lord could easily have lashed out at the sanctimonious crowd. He didn't. He paused, and I'll bet he prayed. And in that prayerful pause, he gave us an example that echoes through the centuries: "Let he who is without sin cast the first stone."

In Jesus' example, we learn to evaluate our angry response and discern whether our anger is justified.

My own unjustified anger sometimes comes when I'm so busy spotting the splinter in someone else's eye that I miss the planks in my own. The incremental effects of my hoarding others' faults can create self-righteousness and resentment. For example, I have a friend who can smell a fault in another human being faster than I can type. This trait irritates me, especially as what he considers to be faults seem so minor. Once when I was cooking dinner, he complained that I didn't grate the cheese in a straight line, but just grated it all willy-nilly and made a mess. I cut a stick of butter in half the wrong way, and—horror of all horrors—I put a carton of milk in the refrigerator without wiping off the lip. I think, truth be told, he needs to work on being more tolerant.

In asking God to grant me a new perspective about this man and help me understand why he gets so exercised over the silliest little things, God didn't say a word about my friend. Instead, God made it clear that I needed to loosen the hold on my own judgments. After all, if I'm so sure that grated cheese, sliced sticks of butter, and milk cartons are of so little consequence, why am I wasting time thinking less of this man for his idiosyncrasies? After all, I have a flaw or two of my own, as God lovingly reminded me.

Grated cheese is a ridiculously trivial example, but the point is important. Our hearts can become hardened when we focus only on people's negative traits. When I became English Department chair a few years ago, a former chair warned me: "Anne Marie, people are going to wear you out. You're going to get tired of all the grief they cause you." I knew he had to be wrong, because I love and respect my colleagues, and I've always felt lucky to spend my days among them.

But he was right.

After a few years on the job, my heart sank whenever certain people walked into my office. I knew they'd come to complain or ask for special treatment or, truth be told, to whine. One year, when the remnants of Hurricane Isabel had severely damaged the Naval Academy, including the English Department's spaces, I was up to my eyeballs in the disaster's aftermath. I was ordering new furniture, checking air quality reports, fussing with temperamental generators, checking for mold growth on the damp walls, attending daily briefings on our recovery status. When a colleague came in to complain about a textbook order that had gone awry, I wanted to throw him out the window. An hour later, I wanted to lash out when someone else walked in and asked me: "When are you going to reorder those pink grade books I like so much? There aren't any in the supply cabinet." But my resentments are my own problem. My colleagues were unaware, as they should have been, of the tremendous strain Isabel had placed on me and my energies.

Of course, we're not called to suffer continually in silence, accepting everyone else's inconsiderate self-absorption. God doesn't call us to be erased by other people. There are times when anger is a God-given response. But flailing about in uncontrolled rage seldom advances the Kingdom. Great saints have struggled with this very issue. Thomas More, who was willing to die for his faith, didn't always control his nastiness; there are astounding records of his cruelty to family members and colleagues alike. John Wesley, a truly holy man, had some rousing battles with his wife. Yet God worked in and through these flawed human vessels.

We need to remind ourselves and others that God is omnipotent and omniscient. We won't be orphaned or abandoned. Horrible things will happen in life: We'll make dreadful mistakes. We'll explode with rage. We'll be abusive. We'll swear. We'll take the name of the Lord in vain. We'll betray and hurt others. We'll get ourselves twisted up in balls of rage. But no single act or series of acts defines us or pushes us away from the God of infinite mercy.

How often have we been told that there's tremendous sorrow in heaven when the saints and angels see one of us give up when we're so close to getting over a hurdle that we felt we simply couldn't jump? Our mortal vision can obscure things for us, so that we truly come to believe that we're defined by our mistakes, defined by the fights we've had. And especially since the sin of anger pits us against other people, we have a ready-made mirror in which to see our ugly distortions.

Because seeing beyond our own misery and grief can be too hard, we become convinced that we're beyond God's mercy. But we never are. Like the thief on the way to Calvary, God can reach us no matter where the despair. We must keep praying, in whatever feeble way we can, no matter how desolate our situation seems.

One of my dearest friends called me last night in a fit of lonely anger. She was having foolish impulses. She wanted to do something—anything—to alleviate the rage and emptiness she was experiencing. Right before calling me, she'd been pounding her fists into a pillow. She called me in desperation and tears.

"Please talk me out of doing something foolish. I don't want to feel the way I'm feeling."

We talked for a little while, and she said: "Okay. I feel a little bit better. Pray for me while I go make myself dinner."

After she'd eaten, she called me back, and we talked and prayed until she felt strong enough to negotiate the rest of the evening on her own.

I use this example with great deliberateness. Our prayers must be woven into the minutiae of our lives, into the daily frustrations and fits of rage and moments of horrendous sadness. Last night was nothing more than an ordinary Monday evening in late March, but my friend was consumed with an anger and loneliness that enveloped her, and she found herself wanting to lash out. By handling the moment through prayer, however, she managed not to succumb to her foolish impulses.

Often our friends sustain us and are the voice of God. A very holy and gifted friend knits prayer shawls for people, and she gave me one for my birthday this year. Hanging on my bedpost, the shawl is a treasure, and I sometimes wrap myself in its softness at night as I sleep. It is made of richly textured wool, in colors that are almost luminescent in their variations of blue and green and magenta and teal and white yarns. When the sun falls on the yarn, the shawl's majestic brilliance shines with an almost jewel-like quality. I took the shawl on a pilgrimage, and we often used it as an altar cloth. Several people took pictures of the shawl and now have photos of it in their albums. Every time I tell my friend how grateful I am for that outward symbol of such grace and prayer, she reminds me: "There is a prayer for you in every stitch. I was praying for you the entire time I made that shawl." What a tremendous comfort.

Our earthly friends are manifestations of a God who loves us.

No matter where we are in our prayer life, in our journeys, we can turn to a God who is right there next to us. A proverbial epitaph memorializes a man who died from a fall from his horse. Written on his tombstone are these words, for all passersby to see:

> My friend, judge not me,
> Thou seest I judge not thee.
> Betwixt the stirrup and the ground
> Mercy I asked, mercy I found.

God's mercy never ends, doesn't dry up. Even as we are falling off our horses to a sudden death, we can call out to a responding God.

We can't see our own situations rightly. For some reason, too many of us feel unloved, unlovable, or unloving. The daily routines of life can be so wearing, but the Christ of Easter Sunday always holds out hope for us. Julian of Norwich's timeless reminder that all shall be well has been passed down to us through the centuries. Both Easter and Julian's reassurances come as a result of suffering. God doesn't remove suffering but fills it with a divine presence. Thus Good Friday precedes Easter. Furthermore, only after God tells Julian that "evil needs must be" does God tell her "all shall be well."

Right now, at this moment, you may be struggling with heavy stones of anger and pain; right now might feel like your Good Friday. But tomorrow, the grief may abate. Right now, you may be in a season of horrendous sorrow and misery—but sorrow and misery won't have the last word.

I grow impatient at times and wish for clearer vision. I wish for the wisdom of eternity. I want to see as God sees. I want to know that the losses I've sustained and the anger I've experienced will be transformed. Lacking eternal vision, I rely on God's promises that he wants us to be happy.

The Book of Sirach offers such encouragement along these lines:

> Study the generations long past and understand;
> has anyone hoped in the Lord and been disappointed?
> Has anyone persevered in his fear and been forsaken?
> Has anyone called upon him and been rebuffed?
> Compassionate and merciful is the Lord;
> he forgives sins, he saves in times of trouble (2:10).

Perhaps there's no larger, more atrocious manifestation of human anger than war. When I visited the beaches of Normandy, I tried to imagine the horror of the invasion, which seemed so remote on that bright summer day. As I stood in the midst of the cemetery, with its rows of white crosses, I thought of the closing scenes of *Saving Private Ryan.* Captain Miller successfully completes his mission to save Private Ryan but is mortally wounded in the process. As Miller breathes his last breaths, knowing that he'll never again see his beloved wife, he whispers into Private Ryan's ear, "Earn this." Miller wants Ryan to be conscious of the cost that has been paid to preserve his life. More subtly, he challenges Private Ryan—and all of us—to make the most of the life God has given us.

Then the movie fast-forwards to Private Ryan as a grandfather, returning to Normandy with his family. Standing beside Captain Miller's grave, Ryan turns to his wife and asks, "Am I good man?" He wants reassurance that he hasn't squandered the second chance he was given, years before, and has been worthy of the sacrifice that so many people made for him. In the context of war, against the backdrop of unfathomable suffering and loss, divine grace seems all the more wondrous. A grace that never says, "Earn this," but reminds us of the Father's gift and the Son's sacrifice. Transforming grace surrounds our every breath. No matter how enraged we are, God beckons us in love.

PRAYER SUGGESTIONS

The Jesus Prayer

Sometimes, at the peak of anger, the slow recitation of the Jesus Prayer has a calming effect. The complete prayer, "Lord Jesus, Son of God, have mercy on me a sinner," requires minimal energy and can bring an immediate sense of the Lord's abiding presence. Even the repetition of only parts of the prayer can replace incendiary feelings and thoughts with a sense of God's love. Prayer gives rage a chance to dissipate. Over and over again, you can say the words, or even one word of the prayer—any one word that will focus your attention on

God. The power of the prayer comes in the name of Jesus. As you clear your mind and spirit of everything but that name and the words of this prayer, the Holy Spirit can permeate your emotions and help your agitation and rage and anger to dissipate.

Praying over an Angry Incident

Praying over past angry incidents may help prevent future ones. What follows is my prayer experience as I prayed over the "spilled-milk" incident described earlier in this chapter. I hasten to add that this prayer was not possible for me until more than a decade after the event. Before then, the searing pain felt too dangerous for me to explore, even in prayer. Now, however, having learned to use this technique, I employ the prayer as close to the event as possible, although such events are almost nonexistent for me now.

In praying over the incident in which I pulled my son's hair, I asked the Lord to help me revisit the scene. I sat in my prayer corner and lit a candle, and then let my mind drift back to the parsonage kitchen, where the incident had occurred. In my mind's eye, I saw again the yellow-and-brown-plaid kitchen carpeting. I saw the glossy brown cabinets above the sink. I asked God to let me look again at the scene, almost as if I were an outside observer. I fully expected to get a harsh view of myself and to have God reprimand me. Instead, God gave me soft eyes and let me see that long-ago distraught young mother, battling desperately with physical and emotional exhaustion. God let me see myself not as some willful harridan intent on harming her beloved son or determined to fill the parsonage with rage. When I saw myself, I actually felt real sorrow for the young woman I was. Not in a self-pitying way, but in a way that allowed me to recognize that great harm had indeed been done to me. As I sat in the prayer corner, I could almost hear Joey's little feet sliding across the carpeted kitchen floor as he pattered into the room wearing his Doctor Denton pajamas. And when the milk spilled to the floor and I grabbed at his blond curls in a rage, it seemed to me that all the grief inside me broke open.

In praying over and remembering the incident, and asking God to help me see it with new eyes, I felt a real softening. Without a doubt, I had been wrong to lash out at my son in anger. But God allowed me to understand how overwhelmed and hurt and desolate and betrayed I really felt.

In revisiting the parsonage kitchen, I realized that Jesus Christ had been there the whole time, standing next to Joey and me. Had I stopped long enough to acknowledge that divine presence, the anger might well have found a more appropriate channel. Reliving the incident made me mindful that Jesus was right there. I didn't see or feel his presence at the time because my rage was so intense.

Now, when anger starts to rise up within me, I take the time to try to find God, right at that very moment. Wherever I am, in whatever company, I remind myself that God beckons me to control the anger and filter my actions through the sieve of divine and ever-present love.

Chapter 3
Praying with a Weary Spirit

The ringing phone on my nightstand startled me from my early-morning sleep. A bleary-eyed glance at caller ID made my stomach turn over as I realized the dean was calling me at an ungodly hour on a Saturday morning, and it couldn't be good news. I didn't want to pick up the phone. When I did, the dean informed me that one of my departmental colleagues, a fifty-four-year-old man in seemingly perfect health, had died unexpectedly in the night. The dean's words made no sense, and my brain and spirit rebelled against what he was telling me. This colleague could *not* be dead. He'd just been teaching the day before, chatting with everyone in the mailroom as he made copies of a writing assignment for his British literature class.

Because I was the department chair, I needed to pass the word to my other colleagues. When I called my associate chair, an Air Force lieutenant colonel, he reacted as I had, with disbelief and denial. We divvied up the list of department members and started making the phone calls.

John, the man who died, had been a gentleman in every true sense. A devoted and adoring husband, he was also a beloved teacher. Hard at work on a trilogy of novels, he was a great lover of music, a man of great faith.

He had been very interested in my writing this book, and one afternoon last fall, he'd talked to me about his own journey of faith.

I was stunned to learn that he viewed sloth as his worst sin. Sloth is a disease of the will, he'd said, an inability to rouse the self to the right kind of activity. Reminding me that Dante makes Satan an ice-bound figure in *The Divine Comedy*, he'd gone on to explain that acedia has sometimes been understood as a lack of energy to do the good or fight the bad. This dear man told me: "Whatever the right good thing of the day is, I often have trouble doing it. I never feel as good as I'm called to be."

I asked him if he kept praying even when he felt as if he weren't doing what God wanted him to do. Without hesitation, he said: "I'd be worse off if I didn't pray, didn't go to Mass. Praying keeps me in touch with the ultimate realities." Affirming that he never lost a sense of God's presence, he hastened to add, "Sometimes God seems farther away than I'd like." We talked about the burden of the sheer repetitive nature of sloth, of all sin. There is no "fixing" the condition, no defining moment when we're cured once and for all. A Milton scholar, he reminded me that in *Paradise Regained*, the temptation takes place in a desert, not a garden. These words made such an impression on me that I found myself remembering them on the weekend of his death.

During that weekend, I needed to gather up the pertinent facts of his academic career for the public-affairs office. In the departmental files, his folder was crammed so full that I needed two hands to pull it out. Out tumbled copies of articles, flyers from academic conferences, acceptance letters for prestigious seminars. Pressed down and overflowing was the paper trail of this man's activity. As I sat at my desk, trying to make sense of what was before me, I thought about our conversation just a few months earlier. "I never feel as if I'm doing enough," he had told me. "I waste too much time listening to music and buying CDs and just not getting any work done."

At his funeral mass in the Naval Academy chapel, he was eulogized by friends and colleagues alike, who cherished his vast knowledge of music, which he'd shared so generously. In all the months since his death, not one person, even in passing, has suggested that he hadn't done enough. His students miss him terribly. His colleagues and friends, and above all his beloved wife, understand that he is irreplaceable. Still, I remember how clearheaded he was in his assessment of his spiritual path.

His own sense of himself as slothful came from a belief that he wasn't doing enough. And, truth be told, sometimes we don't do enough. Even though to others we seem productive and busy, we get lazy on the inside. John's view of his sloth seemed overly harsh to me; however, I am very mindful that he knew exactly what he was telling me. He was aware, as others might not be, of the ways in which he pulled back from doing the next good thing. His understanding of this sin helped me deepen my own limited understanding. His willingness to talk with me about sloth, his willingness to let me write about him are lasting testimonies of his generous spirit. I cannot diminish that generosity by coloring over what he knew to be a stumbling block for him.

In the centuries before the deadly sins were numbered at seven, there was an eighth sin: sadness, or triste, which over the years merged into sloth. It's important here to differentiate between depression and sloth. Depression is a serious medical condition that can stem from biochemical imbalance. Therefore, like any medical condition, depression should never be labeled a sin. There are strategies for alleviating depression, and there are ways depression-prone people can protect themselves. Depression and sloth may be related. They are not, however, one and the same.

Sloth is a deliberate turning away from the joy of God. As author Evelyn Waugh asserts, "The malice of Sloth lies not merely in the neglect of duty . . . but in the refusal of joy."[2] Not only do we refuse joy, but we also refuse to exert the necessary effort to fulfill our duties in the Kingdom of God. We allow ourselves to become apathetic to divine goodness. Perhaps more than any of the other sins, sloth is a sin of habit. We stop praying; we grow careless; we become indifferent. How often have we been told that indifference, not anger, is the real death threat to human relationships? When we're angry, on some level at least, we are actively engaged and passionately care. Our relationship with God is no different. Indifference can be deadly.

Evelyn Waugh warns, as have others, that sloth tends not to be a sin of the very young. Rather, it can be the "last deadly assault of the devil," as we live longer and longer. In bleak terms, Waugh suggests that "it is in that last undesired decade, when passion is cold, appetites feeble, curiosity dulled and experience has begotten cynicism, that sloth awaits us and deters us on our pilgrimage."[2] Many of us grow weary well before we're anywhere near our last decade, however. We pull back our energies and desires, stay home and flip channels, and cut ourselves off from one another and from God. Sloth is really a pulling back, a reluctance, a sense of futility, a feeling that we're not up to the tasks ahead of us. Staying connected to God through prayer can diminish our tendency to shut down and slow down.

Three of the most vibrant examples of strong faith in the Hebrew Scriptures—Moses, Elijah, and Jonah—also fought against their own nature to accomplish great good. Staying in touch with their Creator fueled their missions.

We think of Moses as a larger-than-life example of a man who fulfilled God's work. Still, in Exodus 4:1, the first word Moses utters as he speaks to God is "But."

But?

This great and holy man, whose life we study and admire, pushes back against the Creator, adamantly resists God's clear will, and questions his ability to do what God wants done. It's such a familiar story that we can miss the nuances in the slow unfolding of the narrative. But let's slow down long enough to put ourselves inside Moses' head. At every step of the conversation with God, Moses pulls back. When God offers encouragement or direction, Moses balks. When God gives consolation, Moses dismisses it. Moses, the great patriarch, just wants to be a regular guy. He wants to go home to the safety and comfort of the familiar. He wants an easy life.

When God gives him orders, he tosses back excuses. Who, *me*? he asks. No one will believe me or listen to me. In reply, God performs miracles to change the minds of the most fervent nonbelievers. He changes Moses' staff into a serpent and back again, and turns Moses' hand leprous, then healthy, in quick succession. "If they will not believe you, nor heed the message of the first sign, they should believe the message of the second," God says. "And if they will not believe even these two signs, nor heed your plea, take some water from the river and pour it on the dry land. The water you take from the river will become blood on the dry land."

You'd think anyone armed with such miraculous divine assurances would simply go forth, energized, with security and joy. But not Moses. Instead, he offers yet another excuse: He's not, he insists, much of a public speaker and tells God he's "slow of speech and tongue." The Lord, presumably losing patience, tells the reluctant leader, "Go, then. It is I who will assist you in speaking and will teach you what you are to say."

Realizing that none of his arguments seems to be working, Moses finally, in desperation, pleads, "If you please, Lord, send someone else." But no matter what he tries, he can't weasel out of his duties. Ultimately, Moses does what he needs to do (Exodus 4:13).

In the everyday push of life, we can come to lose heart, we can lose our courage, and we can believe ourselves too flawed to advance the Kingdom of God. We can never be a Moses, we think. But even Moses wasn't a Moses all the time. He recoiled from his obligations. He wanted to do the easier thing. It was only his continual conversation with his Creator that helped him avoid the pitfall of not doing the next good thing.

Then there's Elijah. Elijah is yet another example of a man who feels he can do no more for God. In 1 Kings 19, he sits under a broom tree and prays for death. "This is enough, O Lord!" he complains. "Take my life, for I am no better than my fathers." Elijah has reason to be weary, to think he can accomplish no more. Other prophets have been killed. He's been fleeing for his life. He's walked for an entire day in the desert. Nothing seems worth doing anymore, and he prays for the release of death. Lacking the energy to take one more step, he falls asleep with this death prayer filling his mind.

God, however, who has other plans for Elijah, sends a very persistent angel to awaken the weary prophet. The angel orders Elijah to eat and drink the hearth cake and jug of water that have been provided. He obeys the angel's commands, but that's all the energy he's willing to muster, and he falls right back asleep. The angel wakes him up again and says, "Get up and eat and drink, else the journey will be too long for you." I have always loved the angel's words "Get up and eat and drink . . ." The simplest acts are sometimes the most necessary. Getting up and eating bread and drinking water are fundamental human acts, from which weariness might dissuade us. Knowing that Elijah must not keep falling asleep, wishing for death, God demands, at first, only fundamental tasks from his reluctant prophet. God has a task for Elijah that will never be fulfilled if Elijah remains inert.

Jonah is the ultimate reluctant prophet, hiding from God in the belly of a whale. He ends up there because he tries to avoid doing what God asked him to do. "Go to Nineveh," God demands, but Jonah just wants to stay put (Jonah 1:2). Though he expends fierce energy dodging his duties, when things don't go his way, Jonah fizzles out and prays for death. And when God doesn't cooperate, Jonah repeats his claim, "I would be better off dead than alive." Life, for Jonah, has become too much of a burden and not worth any effort. Like many people, Jonah starts out with vision and energy and passion, but the continued thwarting of his desires depletes his strength (Jonah 4:3).

When we're buried under the weight of our own existence, we can grow so weary of life that we no longer want to breathe. As a friend of mine often says, "I can't even lift my head from the pillow on some days." Moses and Elijah and Jonah are good companions for times such as those, when we need to shore up the resolve to keep going. On some days, in some seasons, to keep moving takes a monumental act of will and faith. We have to remember that even the greatest souls in the Kingdom struggled with weariness and dissatisfaction, with not having enough oomph to undertake the tasks at hand.

For times like these, self-help gurus will give you the same advice the angel gave Elijah: Do one simple task at a time. Get up. Eat breakfast. Brush your teeth. Make the bed. Doing these menial tasks prayerfully and mindfully can help you through the morass of sloth and into a deeper relationship with God. In walking through an airport once, I saw a flyer with a prayer attributed to William Bridge. Clearly, Bridge struggled with sloth as he prayed, "Ah Lord, my prayers are dead; my affections dead and my heart is dead: but you are a living God and I commit myself to you."

The morass of human existence is an inescapable fact of life. Even the most optimistic, who routinely see the glass as half full, admit to stretches when the simple task of living seems pointless. The writer of the book of Ecclesiastes, sometimes called the most cynical book of the Bible, speaks of the dreariness of life, calling it "a chase after wind," proclaiming human activity profitless, and lamenting that everything comes to nothing anyway. All is vanity, the writer declares: work, pleasure-seeking, ill-timed action. Almost every single action in life is coated over with a sense of futility and hopelessness. Ecclesiastes speaks to the universal sense of loss and despair that can stop us in our tracks and makes us ask, "Why bother?" If we see ourselves in the words of Ecclesiastes, even in our sloth we need to turn to God in prayer.

In our sloth, we focus on ourselves rather than on others and on God. Sloth keeps us from being active in our churches, putting extra effort into our jobs, flexing the muscles of our hearts and minds and imaginations. It weakens our ability to love and be the face of God for others. As one's imagination weakens, so does the ability to see the opportunities to do good that are all around. Refusing to hold open the door for our fellow human beings, we deprive both them and ourselves of the vital energy provided by the communion of saints. But talking to God even through the weariness will keep alive the divine flame in us that equips us to do God's will.

On a pilgrimage to Lindisfarne, I experienced a graphic reminder of the need for continued prayer in the midst of extreme weariness of spirit. My fellow pilgrims and I walked across the sands at low tide, following the path that pilgrims had followed for centuries. A bus had carried us to the far side of the island, and we were to make our way back to the "mainland" on foot through the wet sands. The journey was surprisingly arduous. On that gloomy and misty day, a fierce wind threw some of us off balance. We walked barefoot, the way the earliest pilgrims made the trip. As we started off across the sands, one of us decided not to make the journey. Others wondered if we had the stamina to proceed.

One by one, we started off in silence. The walk was extremely slippery and at points appeared dangerous. The wet sand and cold wind made the journey difficult, as there seemed to be no solid ground. Each of us found different ways of negotiating the trek. Several times, I grew so weary that I wanted to stop, but I gained extraordinary comfort and strength from being in the presence of my fellow pilgrims. My bravery might have failed me without them. I gained strength, too, from the unseen pilgrims who had gone before me on this path, as recently as the day before, as long ago as ten centuries earlier. I felt surrounded by a host of spirits, and that feeling sustained me: I was not in this quicksand alone. And talking to God, all along the way, gave me the vision to keep my eyes focused on both the path beneath my feet and the road ahead of me.

When we gathered together after the pilgrimage walk across the Lindisfarne sands, we all chuckled with delighted relief at our success. The glow of the combined sense of accomplishment was palpable. Many of us exchanged self-conscious stories about how we kept remembering the old western movies from our youth, in which person after person died in quicksand. We chuckled as we remembered the customary warning: "Don't struggle. Struggling makes you sink faster." During the pilgrimage walk, more than one of us had a not-too-happy image of ourselves sinking into the quicksand and dying.

But we didn't die. We persevered in prayer and community and completed the journey.

In a subsequent season of my life, when a sense of dread and ennui overwhelmed me, I called one of my fellow pilgrims and told her: "I feel as if I'm sinking into that Lindisfarne sand. It's grabbing at my ankles."

With the clearest wisdom, she asked me, "Well, what did you do when you felt like you were sinking into the sand on the island?"

"I kept talking to God and thinking about all the people who'd been on the walk before me."

"Do you think," she persisted, "that other people have been overwhelmed by these dreadful feelings in life, as you have?"

"Sure," I replied.

"Then, why not do what you did on the pilgrimage? Keep praying, keep your eye focused on the goal, and call on the strength of all the people who've gone before you and are with you in spirit right now."

Her wise words were pitch perfect for me, and they reminded me of the Old Testament conversations between God and the reluctant pilgrims and prophets. The whole journey of faith is a process, and we will—we absolutely will—face those moments when we don't want to proceed. There will be times when, like Elijah, all we want to do is curl up and go to sleep. Yet even as we sleep, and even as we struggle against inertia, God never departs. Even in the middle of quicksand, God remains.

PRAYER SUGGESTIONS

Trading Hearts with Jesus

In a season when weariness overwhelms your spirit, you might pray this prayer, which is an adaptation of one I heard long ago on a retreat video:

> Lord Jesus Christ, please let me borrow your heart today. Mine is weary and seems incapable of doing much good for me or anyone else. Please take my tired heart and carry it with you, then return it to me when you have recharged it. Until my heart is strong again, please allow me to borrow yours. That way I can walk through my day remembering that I carry you within me and I am bringing you to other people.

The Prayer of the "Right Good Thing"

An examination of conscience provides insight during the weary seasons of our lives. First ask God to grant you an abiding sense of divine presence and love, then review your day. Hour by hour, examine your actions to see where you failed in acts of charity. Start with the little things: Were you too indifferent to greet the mail carrier? Did your own inertia keep you from dropping by to see the new neighbor? Were you too lazy to sign the office card for a sick colleague? Then move on to the bigger issues, trying to identify those places where you pulled back instead of stepping forward toward charity and doing God's will. Make sure you take Jesus Christ with you as you review your day, or else the journey will prove too much for you. As you fall asleep, you can vow to embrace the opportunities for charity tomorrow, asking God to help you do the right good thing.

Counting Blessings

A weary spirit dims your ability to see the good you possess. Calling to mind your simple, daily blessings can improve your vision immensely. The improved vision stirs your heart away from lethargy to charity. As you fall asleep, try to list, gently and without effort, the things in your life for which you are grateful. Something as simple as a slice of fresh lemon in a glass of water may be on the list. Maybe the smooth comfort of burrowing under the covers for a nap makes you happy. Perhaps you were lucky enough today to pat a loved one's face or hold a baby. Ask the Holy Spirit to remind you of the good that surrounds you, and let that goodness fill your spirit as you fall asleep surrounded by the communion of saints.

Chapter 4
Praying with a Lonely Heart

"It's not my problem if he's married. His wife can worry about it."

My friend stood in the doorway of my kitchen, sipping bottled water and chatting about her new boyfriend with great joy. "He's so smart. He's great in bed. And funny. We have the most fun together."

"But he's married," I wailed. "What about his poor wife?"

"Oh, don't give me that poor wife bit. She's been ignoring him for years. He's just a paycheck to her. Besides, I like watching men fall in love with me. There's no real harm here. It'll be over before his wife ever catches on."

This friend is stunningly pretty, well educated, professionally successful, and a woman of faith. She appears self-confident and happy. But the psychic hole inside her looms large. In her quieter, less saucy moments, she readily admits: "The only time I feel as if I'm worth anything is when some man is drooling in front of me. I like knowing that I'm valued, even if it's only for sex. I'm sure God isn't so pleased with me, but God's not much help when I'm lonely."

She's not the only one to feel that God alone cannot fill in the emptiness of her life.

I once attended a singles and divorced group at my parish, and most of us agonized about the pain of broken relationships. Every one of us in our small group, at some point in our lives, had been hurt by another's infidelity. We were all keenly aware of the ways individual desires can conflict with commitments and the greater good. Still, before our six-week session was done, a man and a woman in our group had hooked up with each other for a disastrous one-night stand. Their interaction irrevocably altered the dynamics of the group. After the man left our small group, the woman in the couple told us: "I just needed to know somebody wanted me. I wanted somebody to get excited about me." The issue at hand isn't merely one of hormones and lust, although pure animal desire does cause an abundance of sin. But I'm not interested here in wild promiscuity or addiction to pornography, the inordinate physical desire of which the catechisms speak.

What trips up people of faith most often is the yearning for human companionship, a desire to fill the void left when we feel abandoned or lonely or lost. That excessive yearning manifests itself both physically, as we engage in unsuitable sexual activity, and emotionally, when we won't stand still long enough to let the Lord be the Lord of all of life. The church scandals that erupt with too much regularity aren't merely the outward manifestation of unfulfilled sexual desire. They're the manifestation of the deep need for real intimacy, a need that sometimes pushes us in the wrong direction. The British author Christopher Sykes argues that of "the seven deadly sins, Lust is the only one about which all mankind (with few exceptions) knows something from experience."[1] The universality of the sin stems from our deepest human longings, longings that we don't believe God can attend to.

There are times when God doesn't feel like enough. I once heard a counselor tell a woman that Jesus Christ was husband enough for any woman—she should think of Jesus as her spouse, as a nun might do. I don't mean to be blasphemous, but Jesus Christ can't cuddle on a sofa at night or help do the laundry. He won't attend movies, and he can't take his turn at driving during a long trip. The bulbs in the garden will have to be planted without his help, and he's no help at all in the kitchen. I am not being flip. The issue I raise is at the heart of the sin of lust. We long to be connected to another because then we know we are alive, valued, make a difference.

I still carry an image from my high school days that helps me connect loneliness and lust. I was in the basement of the old Terminal Tower in Cleveland at a newsstand buying a Baby Ruth candy bar. A disheveled, middle-aged man in a dirty brown coat picked up the current issue of *Playboy*. With the magazine open to the centerfold, he gently and mindfully rubbed his thumb over the picture. The utter longing and loneliness of that gesture still haunts me. That man, whoever he was and wherever he is now, was not some dirty old man relieving his sexual frustration by looking at pictures of naked women. He was a human being, in need of some softness, some intimacy, a connection to another person. I thought of him years later, when as I graduate student I read *Lady Chatterley's Lover*, thought by some to be a novel filled with nothing but lust. As the intimate connection between Lady Chatterley and Mellors, her gamekeeper, grows, the man stands beneath her window one night. Of this moment, D. H. Lawrence writes: "All hopes of eternity and all gain from the past he would give to have her there, to be wrapped with him in one blanket and sleep, only sleep. It seemed the sleep with the woman in his arms was the only necessity."[2] When I discovered this passage, filled with yearning, I thought of the man in the Terminal Tower.

When we are in prime spiritual shape, aware that we're carrying God, then we tend not to fall prey to intemperate longings for validation by other people. But there are periods and stretches of life when only another person makes us feel alive and valued. I laughed out loud—in scorn, I must admit—when I heard a woman say that on Friday nights, she pops into a small chapel and says: "Hi Jesus. It's date night. I'm here for our date." This woman may be well on the road to sainthood, but my own spirit recoiled as I thought of the loneliness of sitting in a chapel on a Friday evening, instead of snuggling in front of a fire with a beloved partner. I love being attached to other people.

This point was made painfully clear to me as my children left home and my own sense of identity began to falter. My misery when my first child left home stunned me. Because I'd always had a career, it never occurred to me that the hole in my existence would loom so large. Yet as my family started to change shape, radically, I was forced to face a dreadful reality: my existence did not matter to anyone anymore. I hasten to add that my friends and extended family are loving and loyal, and I cherish them beyond imagining. They miss me when I'm gone away for any length of time, and we e-mail and talk on the phone continually. But I'm not the primary person in any of their lives.

Even now, tears form in my eyes as I must admit: I am not of primary importance to anyone on the face of the earth. And though I have finally accepted that reality, the truth still sears my psyche, in much the same way as it does for a widow I recently met. This dear woman, one of my fellow pilgrims on a trip to the Holy Islands of Iona and Lindisfarne, was talking at dinner and assumed that the gathered group of women were all married. In speaking of her husband's death a few years earlier, she told us: "You should all make sure you appreciate what you have. Do you know how many losses there are when you have no husband?" She proceeded to tell us that when her husband died, she started to write down all the losses she suffered, and she stopped at number twenty.

Listening to her brought back painful memories of my own adjustments to being alone. I still stumble when someone asks me, "Who should we contact in case of emergency?" I never know what to say. Sometimes I leave the question unanswered.

People often are stunned when I tell them that lust is my downfall, because I don't strike anyone as being driven by my physical desires. Instead, I have been driven by my desire to be connected to another at all costs. When I've been in the middle of a troublesome relationship, friends have asked me: "What are you getting out of this? The guy's a bum. He's not treating you well." I haven't cared. No matter how flawed a partner might be, I have, in the past, endured because of my need to feel central to someone's life. For too long, on some basic level, I honestly felt that my existence mattered only if someone needed me. With my intellect, I understood that my life in God is of primary importance. Still, on an emotional level, my driving need was to be central to another human being—the way one is with a child or a loving spouse.

One tender memory captures for me this longing. When a dear friend of mine was suddenly called to serve in Iraq, we had to pack up his house quickly and get his belongings into storage. One of his cherished possessions was a beautiful Amish quilt we'd purchased on an autumn trip to Lancaster County, Pennsylvania. As we started to fold it up, I noticed a few of my long, curly, brown hairs on it, and I started to brush them away. He gently stayed my hand and carefully placed the hairs in the fold of the quilt so that they would be there when he returned.

Perhaps to someone else, his gesture would seem silly or unimportant, but to me, the act felt like pure and simple love. The hairs on my head mattered to this man. How casually we always say that God knows even the numbers of hairs on our heads. For me, God's counting the hairs on my head didn't matter as much as knowing that my hairs were tucked safely into a fold of someone's quilt.

This morning's paper has an article about the lack of women in a remote Alaskan town, a place where men lead the rugged outdoor lives they have chosen. These men are vigorous and healthy and doing what they love in life, but they long for companionship, more than a one-night fling. The men speak freely of the emptiness and loneliness and the fear of growing old alone. Certainly, their sexual frustration jumps off the page, but their longing for a lifetime partner comes through more strongly. Sometimes that longing makes us stray from the image of God we carry within us.

Although Jesus Christ speaks very harshly about adultery and divorce, his compassion toward the women caught in the web of sexual misconduct is quite tender. This man, who can curse a fig tree and a Pharisee with equal vehemence, is kindness itself when it comes to sins of the flesh. One can only speculate about how his own sense of loneliness and isolation may have preyed on him. We do know that his most severe temptations came when he was alone. We know that he bemoaned the fact that he had no place to rest his head. We know the agony he felt when his friends abandoned him in Gethsemane. He knew the sting of not mattering to anyone in particular.

The story of the adulterous woman in John 8 is pretty terrifying. What is not terrifying, however, is Jesus' compassionate response to her. His criticism is aimed at those who accuse her. Many times, I've placed myself inside that woman's body and felt the overwhelming fear she must have felt. The prurient nature of her accusers simultaneously repels and fascinates me. "This woman was caught in the very act of committing adultery," the Pharisees tell Jesus (8:4). Their salacious glee, even in translation, jumps from the page. One imagines that the poor woman had only time to wrap herself in her clothes before being hauled away from her lover. The physical and psychic shock would have been dreadful. Pulled from the warmth of her lover's bed, she stands before this harsh group of men. The Pharisees' insistence that they are commanded "to stone such women" must have cut right to her arteries. The stoning process was brutal and methodical and brought on a slow, torturous death. Her very life was on the line because of her carnal sin.

The Pharisees demand an answer from Christ. "Teacher," they say, "this woman was caught in the very act of committing adultery. Now in the law, Moses commanded us to stone such women. So what do you say?" (8:5). Never one to be rushed, Jesus "bent down and began to write in the sand," possibly to give himself time to think and pray about his response; but the ever-impatient Pharisees press him for an answer, so he straightens up and replies, "Let the one among you who is without sin be the first to throw a stone at her" (8:7). As he resumes his writing in the sand, all the men disperse, one by one, beginning with the elders. The terrified woman remains alone with Jesus. She must be feeling some signs of hope at this point, and he does not disappoint. "Go and sin no more," he tells her (8:11). Jesus Christ almost certainly would have looked straight into her eyes as he spoke these words of compassion.

What strikes me is that the woman does nothing but stay in Jesus' presence. She says only three words in response to a question he asks her. Otherwise, she simply remains near him, not unlike the thief on the way to Calvary. There can be little doubt that like the thief, her life changed because of this encounter. She was, presumably, in the bleakest hour of her existence, when her mistakes came crashing down around her. But the act of staying in Jesus' presence transformed her.

This woman is so distanced from us in culture and centuries that the full force of her story may be lost. But she took a huge risk when her physical needs and desires and longings overrode her common sense. It was early morning, the narrative suggests, and perhaps her rational self had told her she was taking a chance by staying overnight—leaving in the dark surely would have been safer. But her clouded judgment created a near disaster, and in the middle of that disaster, Jesus saved her.

Jesus is not a rock thrower. He doesn't hoard the stones of our mistakes and heave them at us. We sometimes think that if we could only get our stones out of the way, we could, like the women at the tomb on Easter, get to Jesus. Truth be told, the stones are already gone. That's not to suggest some narcissistic theology that reduces all transgressions to simple matters that can be easily dismissed. No. We do make egregious and nearly mortal mistakes. We wound each other and ourselves. Human beings stay entrapped in horrible messes of our own making. The greater truth, however, is that God doesn't abandon us in the midst of our self-made messes. God meets us where we are.

Take the woman at the well, whose story is captured in John 4. Emotional upheaval must have been a constant for this woman. Readjusting to five different men must have caused grief. Like the woman caught in adultery, this Samaritan woman, confronted with the truth of her life, chooses not to flee. She stays in the presence of Jesus Christ.

But unlike the "caught woman," she doesn't remain silent when Jesus speaks to her. Although she's startled by his words, she bandies rhetoric with this stunning man who boldly asks her for water. Their conversation takes surprising twists and turns as Jesus—a complete stranger in this remote village—reveals the depth of his knowledge of this anonymous woman, compelling her to go tell people what has happened. Her life-transforming moment occurs when she stays in the presence of the divine love long enough to let grace work in her. She knows perfectly well that she is a sinner; she understands better than anyone what a mess her life is; and surely she feels exposed and humiliated. Still, she doesn't flee in shame. She pays attention to Jesus' words and allows those words to affect her beliefs. This woman, who has been called the first missionary, carries Jesus' message to her fellow Samaritans: "Come see a man who has told me everything I have done. Could he possibly be the Messiah?" (4:29).

She abandons her valuable water jar and hurries to share the good news. If her own sense of unworthiness had stymied her, the message of transforming love wouldn't have been passed on. Unlike the proud Pharisees, whose backs are too stiff to bend, this woman is malleable and receptive. Her willingness to stay in God's presence is vital. Had she scorned the words of Jesus and fled, her life would have been that much poorer.

We can't recapture, at this distance, her whole history. Skimming over her heartache and grief, however, is a mistake. She needn't become purely the mythic "woman at the well." We must stop long enough to think about the years of missteps; the months of wrong decisions; the tears that fell on her cheeks. The woman at the well can teach us many things, the most important of which is the enveloping power of divine love that doesn't turn away because of our mistakes. God sees the divine imprint in each of us and will call forth that imprint, inviting us to fully inhabit our redeemed selves. Remember, too, that this woman was doing nothing out of the ordinary when Jesus Christ pierced through her life. She was getting water, a task she'd performed hundreds of times, perhaps a drudgery she disdained. Certainly she had no idea her life was about to change when she started out from home. But God pierces through the layers of our lives and meets us with love.

Both the woman at the well and the woman caught in adultery remained open to the transforming power of divine love. Both women were lustful, cluttering their lives with people who blocked the path of God. Still, God found a way through to each of them.

Years ago, a friend gave me an old photocopy of a story by Max Beerbohm. Beerbohm writes a dear story about a lustful man, Lord George, who experiences the transforming power of love. "The Happy Hypocrite: A Fairy Tale for Tired Men" captures the tale of a real playboy who excessively drinks and eats and gambles and womanizes. When he falls in love with an innocent young girl, she tells him: "I can never be your wife. . . . Your face, my lord . . . is a mirror long tarnished by the reflection of this world's vanity. . . . That man, whose face is wonderful as the faces of the saints, to him will I give my true love."

Despondent, Lord George goes to a local mask maker and buys a mask of a saint. Thus disguised, he woos and weds his new love. After they'd been happily married, and George's true nature has changed and he is indeed acting out of true love, an old lover shows up. Having discovered his deceit, she demands that he remove the mask. When he refuses, she violently tears off the mask in front of the young bride. Distraught, George refuses to look at his wife, saying only: "Do not look at me. . . . Nor will I ever curse you with the odious spectacle of my face. Forget me, forget me."

His wife responds: "I am bewildered by your strange words. Why did you woo me under a mask? And why do you imagine I could love you less dearly seeing your own face? 'Twas well that you veiled from me the full glory of your own face, for indeed I was not worthy to behold it so soon."

George's behavior had altered his appearance, his essence. Because he acted in love and devotion, his own face came to reflect those qualities. Staying in the company of his good and loyal bride made him the person he had hoped to be. He'd been a cad for years, a reprobate, beyond any redemption, but he took the chance at redemption, and redemption came. No one could force him to embrace love. He had to move toward it.

So, too, with our relationship to God. God doesn't ever force our will. Instead, God offers bottomless love and invites us to respond.

PRAYER SUGGESTION

The Breastplate Prayer of Saint Patrick

Loneliness reinforces one's sense of desolation, of being utterly bereft of companionship. The Breastplate Prayer of Saint Patrick, or the lorica, as it sometimes called, offers amazing spiritual comfort. The words will reinforce in concrete ways your understanding that God surrounds you, wraps you in love, protects you. Often I start my day by reading this prayer at breakfast. I keep a copy on my desk at work and read it as many times as I need to during the day. The prayer has come to us in many different forms, but the overall sense of protection and support conveyed by the words is powerful. Its very length conveys strength, as if you are enveloped by God at every turn. You cannot be empty with such an ever-present God.

For my shield this day I call:
Christ's power in his coming
And in his baptizing,
Christ's power in his dying
On the cross, his arising
From the tomb, his ascending;
Christ's power in his coming
For judgment and ending.
For my shield this day I call:
Strong power of the seraphim,
With angels obeying,
And archangels attending, in the glorious company
Of the holy and risen ones, in the prayers of the fathers,
In visions prophetic
And commands apostolic,
In the annals of witness,
In virginal innocence,
To the deeds of steadfast men.
For my shield this day I call:
Heaven's might,
Moon's whiteness,
Fire's glory,
Lightning's swiftness,
Wind's wildness,
Ocean's depth,
Earth's solidity,
Rock's immobility.
This day I call to me:
God's strength to direct me,
God's power to sustain me,
God's wisdom to guide me,
God's vision to light me,

God's ear to my hearing,
God's word to my speaking,
God's hand to uphold me,
God's pathway before me,
God's shield to protect me,
God's legions to save me:
From the snares of demons,
From evil enticements,
From failings of nature,
From one man or many
That seek to destroy me
Anear or afar.
Be Christ this day my strong protector:
Against poison and burning,
Against drowning and wounding,
Through reward wide and plenty,
Christ beside me, Christ before me;
Christ behind me, Christ within me;
Christ beneath me, Christ above me;
Christ to right of me, Christ to left of me;
Christ in my lying, my sitting, my rising;
Christ in heart of all who know me,
Christ on tongue of all who meet me,
Christ in eye of all who see me,
Christ in ear of all who hear me.
For my shield this day I call:
A mighty power,
The Holy Trinity,
Affirming threeness,
Confessing oneness,
In the making of all—through love.[3]

Chapter 5
Praying with a Prideful Heart

While writing this book, I've endured some good-natured teasing from both colleagues and friends, who kept asking me, "What sin are you working on this week?" In the hallways, in the mailroom, on the way to class, we'd laugh about lust or gluttony or even sloth.

"But, you know," I'd say, "the chapter on pride has me stumped. I'm not sure of the way in."

I've always heard that the failing we believe we lack is the one we probably possess in large measure. People who claim never to experience envy, for example, might be envious in ways they do not recognize. Though I have always understood this intellectual concept, I was quite certain that I was aware of my own weak spots. And I knew, without a doubt, that pride wasn't a stumbling block for me. After all, here I am writing about my own failings and weaknesses, offering up for public consumption the bleakest moments in my life.

But in two humbling and separate incidents, God shook me into a deeper truth, forcing me to accept the true nature of my own sinful pride.

The first occurred in the middle of a conversation between God and me. Trapped in yet another dreadful meeting of department chairs, I should have been listening to the dean and his PowerPoint presentation. Instead, my spirit was half a world away. The dean was discussing a critical point about the future of the Naval Academy, and as English Department chair, I should have granted him my full attention. I tried to look interested as I sat there in the uncomfortable and ugly orange chair, but I just didn't care about what he was saying.

Instead, I was mentally replaying an earlier, frustrating conversation with a dear friend, a man who steadfastly and adamantly refuses to trust and love other people. For months, I'd made him a spiritual project of sorts: I was determined to encourage him to realize that love is more important than anything else; to help him understand that he was of inestimable worth.

Now I angrily asked God: "Why can't he understand how important love is? How valuable he is? His parents love him. His siblings adore him. His colleagues respect him. His friends can't wait to see him and hear from him. He's funny and tenderhearted and smart and adorable. God, why can't he figure out that he's fighting imaginary demons and he is very precious to you?"

As I sat there fussing and fuming, God gave me a blunt and pointed response: "Why don't you understand how much I love you?"

I almost stood up out of my chair, the words were so direct.

And I understood immediately what I was being told. I understood immediately.

The months I'd spent trying to enlighten this man were not motivated purely by my love for him, although that was the story I told myself. Those months could have been better spent letting myself experience God's love, coming to understand, again and again, that I am loved beyond all measure by God. As long as I focused on another human being, who seemed spiritually stagnated, I avoided doing my own spiritual homework. The splinter in his eye loomed so large that I didn't see the plank in my own. I don't mean to suggest that my efforts to love this friend were invalid, or that he wasn't in need of a healthy dose of affirmation, but I was spending far too much time worrying about his spiritual welfare. My tacit starting point was my superior position.

God clearly wanted to recalibrate my thinking.

Within weeks of this experience, still smarting from the realization, I met another fellow who seemed so spiritually smug that he rankled me profoundly. A man of faith, he quickly began pointing out what he perceived to be my spiritual myopia. I'd tell him about a spiritual idea, and he'd say, "Well, I'll have to pray that God gives you a better vision." I'd talk about a passage in Luke that caught my eye, and he'd correct me: "No, what that really means is . . ."

At first, I couldn't understand why his attitude bothered me so much. After all, I'm always hungry for spiritual conversation, eager to discover like-minded pilgrims who will talk about God in ways that suit my temperament and spiritual inclinations. But then it dawned on me: I didn't like being talked down to. I didn't like someone else suggesting that he had a better handle on God than I did; that his was the greater, mine the lesser vision. I didn't like this man treating me as I had treated my dear friend—as someone who didn't quite "get it."

"Who are you," I asked him once in anger, "to presume to tell me that my vision of God is flawed? Who are you to tell me that God speaks to you in ways that God does not speak to me? I've been doing pretty well without you for years, thank you very much, so leave me alone."

And you know who I sounded like?

And do you know what I sounded like? A Pharisee. One of that proud and spiteful and spiritually hardened tribe that refused to allow the love of Jesus to work in their lives.

In these two conversations, I was made to realize that I don't want my view of God, or my path to God, challenged by anyone or anything. God has been at the center of my whole life, more or less, and I'm accustomed to being the default "God person" in any group. My relationship with God has changed and deepened over the years. Filled with ups and downs, fertile and sterile stretches, my faith journey has been the North Star of my existence. People who know me also know that God matters to me. After all, I was a minister's wife for twenty-four years. Before that, I was in a convent. The record of my life shows a pattern of at least outward interest in matters spiritual. Even now, as a grown woman, I always chuckle at what I call the *Sound of Music* phenomenon. When people discover that I was going to be a nun, even though it was decades ago, they suddenly think of me as Maria von Trapp.

Never did I think that my spiritual journey was a source of sinful pride, never did I think of myself as a Pharisee, until the two incidents in which God granted me greater insight.

The Pharisees have always fascinated me, ever since childhood. They came in such clearly labeled "bad-guy" costumes, and they were always good for a story. Even as a kid, when I started to nod off during the reading of the Gospel, my ears perked up at the mention of the word *Pharisee.* They were always getting in trouble, and Jesus was always yelling at them. Like the sometimes obtuse Saint Peter, they were always good for a dose of spiritual dim-wittedness. Even as a child, I came to understand that I was better than a Pharisee.

Not until I discovered that some scholars believe that Jesus himself was a Pharisee did I begin to rethink my view of them. Given that Judaism was divided into sects during Jesus' time, the assumption is that the Savior had to emerge from one of them. One school of thought argues that the man from Nazareth was so hard on the Pharisees because, as one of them, he knew them and their foibles well. Their pride and stiff necks were piqued by Jesus' assumption that they were missing something vital in their understanding of God. They knew the rituals and regulations of religion, but they didn't know or live the love of God.

Someone once scoffed, "The Pharisees narrowed the 10 Commandments to 113," highlighting the way they observed the law. It's easy for us to chuckle at their narrow-mindedness, but in their own day, the Pharisees were the moderate Jewish voice. Unlike the Sadducees, who were pro-Rome and learned to use the Roman occupation to their advantage, the Pharisees were separatists who refused to embrace foreign rule. They weren't as revolutionary as the Zealots and certainly not as ascetic as the Essenes, who lived like monks.

So for this fairly moderate group, being accused of narrow-mindedness and spiritual stagnation by one of their own must have been a source of enormous anger and generated tremendous hard-heartedness. When Jesus initially rose to prominence, the Pharisees may have thought they'd be part of his inner circle. When he started attacking their views of themselves, they were unable to accept his words. A lifetime of thinking of themselves as the "spiritual experts" had hardened their hearts.

That hardening did not happen all at once. The Pharisees didn't start out turning their backs on Jesus, on God. They didn't start out listening only to their own voices. Raised in the Jewish faith, they incorporated God into the very fabric of their lives. They were people of prayer, of deep faith. But along came Jesus to challenge them and push them out of their comfort zones—and their backs stiffened and their pride kicked in, and they lost the chance to be transformed by love.

The New Testament is rife with stories about the Pharisees. Chapters 5 and 6 of Luke's Gospel narrate a particularly telling incident. A Pharisee named Simon invites Jesus to dinner. The invitation itself is startling, for the Pharisees, as a whole, had decided that Jesus needed to be contained. They'd become "frenzied and began asking one another what could be done to Jesus" (6:11). Surely some of Simon's friends had cautioned him against inviting the troublesome Jesus to his home, for the Pharisees had already endured too much indignity at his hands. They repeatedly asked testy questions: "Who is this man who utters blasphemies? Who can forgive sins but God alone? (5:21). "Why do you eat and drink with tax-collectors and non-observers of the law?" (5:30). "Why are you doing what is prohibited on the Sabbath?" (6:2). Jesus steadfastly answers them:

"Why do you harbor these thoughts?" (5:22). "I have not come to invite the self-righteous to a change of heart but sinners" (5:32). "Have you not read what David did when he and his men were hungry—how he entered God's house and took and ate the holy bread and gave it to all his men, even though only priests are allowed to eat it?" (6:2). At each turn, when the Pharisees pipe up with a self-important or self-righteous question, Jesus pointedly answers them. They feel increasingly marginalized and threatened.

So for Simon to invite Jesus into his home in this climate is an act of faith. But when Jesus behaves in unorthodox fashion, Simon recoils, seemingly rejecting what is offered. I can imagine Simon talking with Jesus at the beginning of the meal, trying mightily to uncover the true nature of this supposed prophet. I can see the table cluttered with food and hear the easy banter of voices, as people mingle and enjoy one another's company. The Pharisees in attendance might even be thinking that they've misjudged this Jesus—that perhaps he is, after all, one of them. Maybe they can convince their fellow Pharisees that Jesus isn't really a threat at all. He's just one of them.

And then, amid the chatter and camaraderie, the unexpected and unthinkable occurs. A known sinner walks into their midst.

One by one, they all stop chewing. They put their wine glasses on the table. Perhaps the musician is signaled by the host to stop playing. Once they spot the sinner, some of them likely try to push her back outside. She doesn't belong.

What courage it takes for her to weep in front of that group, with their thick animosity filling the air. How persevering she is to drop to her knees and kiss Jesus' feet. As she wipes them with her hair and perfumes them with oil, she can hear the men talking above and around her, expressing disdain and disgust, but she continues in love.

Jesus doesn't pull away.

The Pharisees do.

Simon tells himself, "If this man were a prophet, he would know who and what sort of woman this is that touches him—that she is a sinner" (7:39). The Pharisees believe that they know how prophets should behave. The woman kneeling at Jesus feet doesn't deserve to be in their presence, let alone the presence of a prophet. Simon and his friends believe that they possess specific knowledge about the workings of God, but they can't recognize God in their midst. Their need to exert their own sense of superiority over the woman and Jesus is paramount. Certainly, they know they are better than the woman. That assumption is not even worth questioning.

And that's how pride works, in these small, insidious ways.

We come to believe we're better than others. We take God's good gifts and use them as proof that we're superior. A mother with well-behaved and productive children harbors the tacit belief that she did a better job of mothering than her friend whose children are always in trouble. The man who becomes a CEO while his college roommate gets stuck in middle management assumes that he's worked harder and done the right things to get ahead. The academic who is made full professor while some of her colleagues get stuck in lower ranks knows full well that she deserves the promotion because her efforts have been exemplary.

Each of us has a pride, a vanity that puffs up our own sense of who we are. If we're in good shape, we disdain those who don't work out. If we make healthy food choices, we look askance at those who stuff their mouths with Hostess Twinkies. If we've managed our money well and have a comfortable nest egg, we're certain we're better than those who spend all they earn. If we keep the insides of our cars immaculate and our homes spotless, we have all the proof we need that we're better than those who can't be bothered to keep their surroundings tidy.

Such behavior fits almost perfectly the classic catechism definition of pride as the inordinate desire for self-esteem. As the Jesuit author John Hardon writes, "The problem is that we tend to forget who God is and who we are. . . . The further problem is that we not only tend to take other people for granted, and forget how much we owe to everyone whom God has put into our lives, but we are slow to recognize the good qualities of others and become preoccupied with ourselves."[1]

Such a preoccupation leads to a gradual hardening of heart.

A dear friend of mine loves to tell the story of how to boil a frog to death, and the anecdote bears repeating here. The trick, he says, is to plop the frog into a pot of room-temperature water, then slowly raise the heat bit by bit. The frog, unaware of the incremental rise in temperature, stays in the water until the heat is fatal. If you put a frog directly into scalding water, it would immediately bolt, recognizing the danger. It's a crude example, but so, too, does the gradual hardening of our hearts become spiritually lethal by degrees.

Literature swells with examples of proud and boastful characters. Christopher Marlowe's Dr. Faustus comes to mind, a man so proud of his learning that he seeks immortality and wants to assume God-like powers, selling his soul to achieve even more knowledge and power. In the end, he's hounded into hell. Larger than life, Faustus is a grim and gruesome example of sinful pride at which we can point, keeping ourselves at a safe distance as the hellhounds drive him to damnation.

But sometimes pride wears a more agreeable face.

Enter the romantic and smooth Mr. Darcy from Jane Austen's *Pride and Prejudice.* Wealthy and independent, he falls in love with Elizabeth Bennett, whose father's wealth and status can't possibly match his own and whose mother is a scatterbrained busybody. To make matters worse, some of her sisters are silly and inconsequential. When Mr. Darcy, almost against his will, proposes marriage to Elizabeth, he mentions "his sense of her inferiority" and his fear that marriage to her would be "a degradation." Elizabeth refuses his proposal, berating him: "From the very beginning, from the very first moment I may almost say, of my acquaintance with you, your manners impress[ed] me with the fullest belief of your arrogance, your conceit and your selfish disdain of the feelings of others." Darcy and Elizabeth are locked in a battle of wills. Though truly drawn—and perfectly suited—to each other, each has a preconceived notion of what love and marriage might look like. In their obdurate refusals to see clearly, both almost lose a great love.[2]

When Saint Augustine argues that we can love and do what we will, he carries us right to the heart of God. Almost every sin reflects a failing on our part, through hard-heartedness or woundedness, to enter fully into the love that God offers. Every time we rise up and exert our hard will, we lose yet another opportunity to be who God has created us to be.

In losing these small opportunities, we run the risk of being like the proud Pharisees. We share their blind arrogance. For me, the discovery of my own affinity with the Pharisees has been an unpleasant but necessary shock to my spiritual awareness. I admitted earlier in these pages my realization that I cling too readily to other people. What an unpleasant discovery it was that I also cling too much to my own sense of spiritual understanding.

PRAYER SUGGESTION

Praying with Soft Eyes

Horseback riding requires the rider to develop "soft eyes," a phrase coined by Sally Swift in her book *Centered Riding*.[3] It refers to the need to develop peripheral vision. If the rider stares too intently at an object on the path, or even at the horse's head, the horse can feel the tension. The rider's body becomes stiff and hard and strained, and the horse responds in kind. But if the rider instead focuses loosely on an object, taking in the surroundings, the body relaxes, and the horse follows suit.

Say, for example, the rider spots a log on the bridle path and immediately focuses on the log as a stumbling block and safety threat. Rider and horse will both tense, and the log becomes a real obstacle. If, instead, the rider, upon spotting the log, softly looks at it and the wider landscape, allowing her peripheral vision to absorb the sky and the ground and the neighboring trees, both rider and horse remain calm.

When troublesome people become logs on your path, try to look at them with soft eyes, asking God to allow you to see them as God sees them. Try not to stare intently at them, noticing their every flaw and weakness. Rather, try to hold them in your vision and your heart with the same softness that God extends to you. And then pray for them, as praying for others softens both your eyes and your heart.

Chapter 6
Praying through the Emptiness

The beer can pyramid was the biggest joke in the dorm. Susan, a college freshman, stacked them on her third-floor windowsill, and we all chuckled as the pyramid got higher and higher. She boasted that she had consumed the beers right there in her room, even though she was underage and drinking was prohibited on campus. Because no one ever saw her drink the beer, little could be done to curb her drinking. As a college junior and the dorm counselor on the floor, I saw no real harm in Susan's playful pyramid.

Years later, after alcoholism had ruined Susan's life, I had a conversation with her mom.

"None of us knew," her bereaved mother said. "We had no way of knowing how insidious alcoholism is. All those beers weren't a joke. We just thought they were."

Looking back on those years when I was a dorm counselor to scores of freshman girls, I realize that many of them used alcohol and sex to stave off their fear and loneliness. At the time, my own inexperience and lack of wisdom rendered me pretty useless. I could listen to them talk about their escapades, I could offer help and advise caution, but I couldn't see what they were really fighting.

One of the freshmen, with a sexual assurance that absolutely mystified me, announced one day when she plopped down in my dorm room: "Whenever I want to sleep with someone, all I do is go to the library or the cafeteria. Guys are so superficial. They practically start panting when they see me. So if I get lonely or bored, I get dressed, put on makeup and perfume, and hit the book stacks."

I stammered out the obvious question: "Aren't you afraid of getting pregnant or picking up some disease?"

"Oh, I'm very careful about that stuff," she said. "I know what I'm doing."

A friend of mine has always struggled with her weight. When she was a child, her mother padlocked the refrigerator to keep her from overeating. As an adult, she's gained and lost thirty pounds or so more than once. This woman knows that her overeating masks some real emptiness within, but she's at a loss to figure out what that emptiness might be.

It took me a few decades to realize that alcohol and sex and food are only three of the more obvious ways we try to stave off the sheer terror of being human, of being unable to confront the abyss of our own perceived emptiness. Traditionally, the sin of gluttony encompasses an inordinate use of created things, a lack of temperance. The very fears that lead us to overuse anything can propel us even farther away from our own God-given goodness. We become so entrapped by the food or the sex or the alcohol or the activity that we forget we're made in God's image. We even forget that we're carrying God.

The traditional understanding of gluttony, as author Patrick Leigh-Fermor writes, suggests that there are five ways of committing this sin: "Too soon, too expensively, to much, too eagerly, and making too much of a fuss."[1] Clearly, the sin involves overindulgence in many good things, not just food or wine.

Sometimes seemingly little signs hint at our lack of temperance, our inability to curtail our consumption. One acquaintance of mine forever orders things from catalogs. "It makes me so happy," he tells me, "to know there will be a package waiting for me when I get home. I always like knowing that something is coming in the mail."

Every day he receives more catalogs, as he's added to more and more mailing lists. He lives alone and tells me with delight: "When I sit down to eat at night, I flip through the catalogs, then order stuff. And these companies have twenty-four-hour service, so sometimes if I can't sleep, I call and order stuff at two or three in the morning. That way at least there's a live person to talk to."

Every workaholic I've ever known is running from emptiness. The running may be masked as devotion to duty or commitment to charity; whatever the reason, workaholics glut themselves on work. Some jobs are more demanding than others, to be sure, but we all know people for whom work becomes a dodge for doing the real work of living and loving. One of my former colleagues, a man with deep-down tenderness, always disparaged other faculty members who weren't at work late at night the way he was. "What are they doing goofing off," he'd ask, "when I'm here night after night so late?" The truth, obvious to anyone paying attention, was that this man didn't know how to create a life for himself. So he filled his hours with work.

During one stretch of my life, I'd go see almost every movie Hollywood churned out—from *Austin Powers* to *Shakespeare in Love*—to avoid going home to an empty house at dinnertime, that time of day I call the witching hour. My routine was set. I'd leave work early enough to rush to a twilight showing, thus snagging a cheap ticket. I'd order popcorn, chocolate-covered raisins, and a soft drink. I'd sit in the last row, in the corner, up against the wall, and I'd get lost in the screen. Once the previews started, I'd settle into my seat, content and happy to be distracted for a few hours. Fortified by this ritual, I could then go home and walk into my empty house.

The seeming emptiness of my home terrified me, an emptiness that overindulgence seeks to keep at bay.

Even a cursory review of my own life reveals the stuff I've forced into my daily routine to avoid emptiness. I've sometimes been so busy that even I couldn't keep up with myself, and each of those patches in my life has been a marked period of spiritual desolation, periods when I've lost my way. I was incapable at such times of feeling God's love or responding to God's grace—my terror of loneliness was too great.

I'm only half joking when I tell my firstborn son that when he left home, I replaced him with a horse. While it's true that having one child leave home gave me more time to pursue horseback riding, it's also true that the gaping hole of this boy's departure made me feel desolate. Several years later, when my whole family had changed shape, I bought a piano. A horse and a piano may seem far different than too much alcohol and sex, but the fear of the empty space and the attempt to fill it are the same.

My friends and family always tried to reassure me lovingly that my sense of emptiness was self-imposed. One night, when I was weeping to my sister Charlotte, I said with some vehemence, "I'm so tired of living in this empty house by myself." Without taking a breath, she quietly and firmly responded, "It's not empty." When a dear friend of mine, a steady companion and a naval officer, was deployed to Baghdad, he tried to calm my fear of his impending departure by telling me: "Anna, you are not alone. Even though I'm gone, I'll be right here with you." Another friend always summons the heart to end our long phone conversations by saying, "I love you." My world brims with goodness and abundance, but sometimes I'm so busy worrying that I am blind.

There's nothing wrong with alcohol or sex or food or mail-order catalogs or movies or work or horses or pianos. They can all be God-given gifts to enjoy, and you could argue that part of being human is finding ways—such as horseback riding or piano playing—to get through the rough patches in life. Yet when we overdo it, using activity and things to stuff the holes in our lives, we miss an opportunity to recognize the abundance we already possess.

An incident in the Gospel of Matthew draws attention to our fear of emptiness. The temple tax collectors, harassing Peter, ask him, "Does your teacher not pay temple tax?" Jesus, in an attempt to soothe a potentially volatile situation, tells Peter, "Go to the sea and cast a hook; take the first fish that comes up, and when you open its mouth, you will find a coin; take that and give it to them for you and me" (17:24–27).

This particular type of fish, now known as St. Peter's Fish, carries its fertilized eggs in its mouth. Once the baby fish hatch, they swim out of their parent's mouth to start life on their own. But the parent fish, in an attempt to fill the empty space, stores other objects in its mouth—small rocks, bottle caps, bits of broken plastic, even coins. Routinely, odd bits and pieces of trash are found in the mouths of these fish. The coin Peter finds in the fish's mouth is a replacement for a missing baby.

From the beginning, human existence has been marked, in part, by our use of gluttony to fill the perceived void of being alive. Consider John Milton's depiction of the Fall in *Paradise Lost.* Eve doesn't take a dainty bite from the apple. She gorges herself. She stuffs her face. In my mind's eye, I'd always pictured her taking a little nibble, perhaps like Snow White, and immediately feeling the effects. But that's not the picture Milton paints. In addition, he offers a bit of a back story that suggests why Eve may be so ready to fall into the sin of gluttony: she and Adam have been arguing.[2]

Milton's epic offers up prime proof of what I always tell my students: we read literature, in large measure, to understand ourselves. *Paradise Lost* gives us ample opportunity to travel back and think about why the first humans turned away from God: Like us, they wanted more than they got. Like us, they felt a void in their lives and they wanted to fill it.

The two creation accounts in Genesis don't offer such insight, and part of Milton's genius is his ability to fashion Adam and Eve and Satan into very real, believable characters. We can learn a lot by taking a close look at the Ninth Book of Milton's Christian epic. It shows, for example, that our trespasses do not occur in a vacuum—

our decisions both affect and are affected by others. It shows that when we're tempted, we become blind, as Eve did, to the abundance that already surrounds us. And perhaps most important, it shows that a persistent, determined Satan, resolved to ruin all that is good, just as he entrapped Adam and Eve, can entrap us too. If we don't pray, we're sitting ducks for his wiles.

In Milton's account, the Cherubim, warned that Satan might try to force his way onto the earth, stand guard to protect Adam and Eve. But Satan finds a circuitous route that bypasses their watchful eyes: he slinks into a river and rises in the mist, and evil enters life at its source—water—in the body of a snake. From this lowly position, Satan is overcome with awe, and then grief, at the heavenlike beauty of earth. His admiration quickly turns to hatred, however, and he determines to ruin what he sees. "For only in my destroying I find ease," he explains, "to my relentless thoughts."

At the same moment that Satan arrives, amazed and grieved, Adam and Eve are in the midst of a marital dispute. Eve complains to Adam that all their gardening is to no avail because "the work under our labor grows." Her concern is the same as every gardener's: no matter how hard the two of them work, they can't keep the weeds under control. Her solution: divide and conquer. She suggests that she and Adam work separately, doubling their efforts. Working together, she argues, is distracting; splitting up will make them more efficient.

Adam, however, is reluctant to let her go. They've been warned about the "malicious Foe," and he doesn't want Eve to fall victim to Satan. Naturally, Eve balks at the suggestion that her weakness makes her vulnerable. She prevails, and off she goes to her own little corner of the garden.

Satan, delighted to discover her alone, he pulls out all the stops. He flatters and cajoles and wheedles until he persuades Eve to eat the apple. "Meanwhile," Milton writes, "the Hour of Noon drew on, and wak'd/An eager appetite, rais'd by the smell/So savory of that Fruit."

Milton's depiction of sin is multifaceted. Several factors are working in Eve: she's hungry; she's vain; she's still a bit miffed at Adam. The Devil plays to her multiple weaknesses. Like Eve, when we stumble, we seldom do so in isolation. Many factors are weighing on us, psychically tugging at our will and our common sense.

So when Eve finally does eat that apple, she's ravenous: "Greedily she ingorg'd without restraint/And knew not eating Death." Knowing she's been a glutton, she gets testy when she returns to Adam. The fundamental nature of their relationship changes because of her transgression.[3]

Two biblical stories—one in the Hebrew Scriptures and one in the Christian—cast an interesting light on gluttony. Like the real-life and literary discussions of the sin, they suggest that something else is always at play when human beings indulge in excess. They highlight the fact that our attempts to fill the void have repercussions. Almost always, there is a ripple effect. One gluttonous act can harm not only oneself, but others as well.

Genesis depicts a family that contemporary observers might call dysfunctional: the family of Jacob and Esau. Sibling rivalry. A mom and a dad who play favorites. Power struggles. All the makings of a drama with an unhappy ending. And the trouble begins even before the twins are born: their mother, Rebekah, laments that the children in her womb jostle each other so much. Not surprisingly, Esau and Jacob develop into two totally different personalities. Rebekah prefers Jacob, while the father, Isaac, prefers Esau. If the writer gave us no more details than these, we'd know this family was headed for peril.

Jacob and Esau must have grown up knowing that their parents didn't love them equally. So it's easy to imagine the anger that erupts the day Esau demands some stew from his younger brother. Jacob, the homebody, has been cooking, while Esau, the outdoorsman, has been out in the fields. When Esau comes inside, famished, he demands: "Let me gulp down some of that red stuff. I'm starving" (25:30).

As vibrant as the words *gulp* and *starving* are, it's hard to believe this young man is in any imminent danger of malnutrition. He may be hungry, but his peremptory demand reveals other dynamics at work: his fierce need to have his needs met; his desire to establish authority over his brother; his longing for control.

When Jacob, the younger twin, responds, "First give me your birthright," Esau, aghast, replies, "Look, I'm on the point of dying." But Jacob, with a fierce hunger of his own, insists on his price for a plate of stew. "Swear to me first," he says, and Esau, more interested in food than birthrights, acquiesces and eats his fill (25:31–34).

The incident is brief but nonetheless telling. Neither boy is acting his best. Both are letting their gluttony muddy their behavior. Esau's gluttonous demand for his brother's lunch, mindless of the consequences, serves as an example of what can happen when we rashly reach out to fill a hole in our existence that might be fixed in better ways than with "fast food."

I once heard someone argue that we should keep the word *HALT* in mind as we barrel through life. We should never allow ourselves to become too hungry, too angry, too lonely, or too tired. If we do, we're more likely to fall prey to temptation. Esau's intemperate desire for food makes both him and his brother behave recklessly. The results of their actions plague them for the rest of their lives.

Fast-forward to the story of the Prodigal Son. We don't know if the dissension between the two brothers in this story started before birth, but trouble breaks out when the dissolute son returns home after wasting his inheritance. His father's merciful welcome rankles the more temperate brother. We don't know how the family drama played out in the long run, but no doubt the foolish excesses of the prodigal son made the family circle an unhappy one

Here the excesses seem to be born of a restless spirit, an unwillingness to stay put and find the joy in living an established life among family and friends. The story suggests that the wayward son is a thrill seeker who eats and drinks too much and spends time with "loose women." It's easy to imagine the life the absent son led when he was far from home, with rich food, indiscriminate sex, and wild parties—all meant to fill the time and waste away the hours. Only when desperation sets in, when he realizes he's at the end of his resources, does he think of home—not lovingly or with remorse, but with self-pity: "How many hired hands at my father's place have more than enough to eat," he reflects, "while here I am starving" (Luke 15:17).

By the time he resolves to head homeward, he has acknowledged his failings, but his initial thoughts of home were prompted by the same emptiness that made him abandon his family in the first place. His life abroad hadn't filled up the void, and eating too much hadn't granted him peace. He was fortunate enough to have come to his senses before death caught up with him, but not before he'd brought misery to himself and his family.

When Jesus told this story, his listeners must have been shocked. Asking for an inheritance, in essence, is asking for a father's death—such an unthinkable request would dishonor the father. Even more shocking, the father grants the request. Then the son breaks Talmudic law by traveling to a distant country. When things go wrong, he bonds himself to a pig farmer, working even on the Sabbath, turning against his father in every important way and mocking everything the man holds dear. But when the boy nears home, his father, breaking all convention, runs to greet his wayward child. He gives the boy his shawl and signet ring, and he throws a lavish feast (15:20–32).

Compassion is at the heart of this parable. The son has done almost everything wrong he could have, yet his father welcomes him home with love.

Jacob and Esau and the Prodigal Son are outsize examples of overindulgence. It's easy to keep their stories at arm's length, because most of us haven't traded birthrights for stew or squandered our early inheritance. But the young men in these stories probably didn't start out with larger-than-life gluttony. Bit by bit, they made choices that got them in deeper and deeper, until eventually they were in over their heads.

Sometimes I consume Pepsi and Oreos in alarming quantities. That detail might seem totally unimportant. But consider this detail: when all seems well in my world, I can leave the cookies and soda alone. I'll make a mad dash to the store to buy these sugary foods, though, when I'm faced with a troublesome writing deadline. In some mysterious way, the food helps stave off the terror of facing an empty page. Fortified by an unhealthy overdose of sugar and caffeine, I can turn back to writing and fill up that blank space. At the moment my writing sticks, I don't stop to pray or recollect that God is right here with me in my study. No, I get fidgety and feel barren and not at all prolific. Like a St. Peter's fish, I stuff trash into my mouth to make up for the emptiness I feel.

A good and gracious God reminds me again and again that my sense of emptiness, although real, is not true. God is right here. As Gerard Manley Hopkins says, "The world is charged with the grandeur of God." If I stay mindful and place every activity under God's protection, there's no need to panic, and I'm much less likely to run to the convenience store for sweets when writer's block hits. For me, Pepsi and Oreos are the little symbols of the larger problem, the greater fear. Some days I simply don't feel brave enough to negotiate life on my own. My challenge is to avoid letting such days accumulate; to talk to God even in the midst of them and respond to the abundant grace of the Creator.

Even in the perceived emptiness, we must remain open to God's transformation, not working on ourselves so much as allowing our Creator to work in us. As long as we leave one tiny crack open, God can work wonders. If we stay in Jesus' presence, like the woman caught in adultery, we will grow in love and into the people we're called to be. Nothing we do can withdraw divine love; God acts in us whether we know it or not. God's grace works on us even when we are not open to it or "listening" for it. Prayer—even as we gorge ourselves in ways that are unhealthy—helps us stay open and makes us more mindful of God's presence. God suffuses the whole of life, even our suffering, even our mistakes.

That's the best news. We're all in this struggle together, but God is closer than our next breath. God *is* our breath. When we go to church, we're attending a hospital for sinners, and each and every one of us is a patient. Being present in church, like being present in prayer, deepens our willingness to allow God to transform us. We're not hypocrites if we pray and attend church before reconciling our differences with others. The Gospels encourage us to try to seek forgiveness, to try to mend our ways, before placing our sacrifices on the altar. But they don't say we have to get everything all squared away before we can approach God. Hubert Van Zeller, in *A Book of Beginnings*, writes:

> Say you spend a morning with a man exchanging thoughts about prayer, and a few hours later you see the same man thrown out of a bar, woefully drunk. If your prayer has taught you anything, you do not say, "What business has that hypocrite to talk about the spiritual life?" Instead you say, "How strongly grace must be working in him if in spite of his drinking he is evidently attracted to prayer . . . and if he had not the prayer life behind him now how much drunker he would be."[4]

We are not hypocrites when, as sinners, we persist in prayer.

The joy of life comes in the ongoing awareness of an indwelling God, who surrounds and enfolds and protects and encourages us, at every single step along the way. We're not locked into mortal combat with our depraved and fallen selves. Rather, we are, like the young Jesus in the temple, about our father's business, carrying God into the world.

On a pilgrimage to the holy island of Lindisfarne, God's abundant grace so overwhelmed me that my own breath caught on the wind. After dinner one night, I walked down behind Saint Mary's Priory, the island's medieval church. I walked past a grazing dark brown mare, then down to the beach, where I stooped to collect shells for a friend back home. With a handful of shells, I walked up onto an adjacent hill, and turned to look at the sunset. The mare was still grazing in the pasture below. Behind her, the sun was setting over the North Sea, casting pink and purple and blue rays into the late-evening clouds. Off to my right, sheep were nibbling at the grass. Saint Mary's Priory was in my direct line of vision. The view was breathtaking.

From out of nowhere came a rush of loving voices, seemingly carried on the evening air. Woven together were the spoken reassurances of my friends and family: "You are not alone." "Your house is not empty." "I love you." I felt the immediate presence of my maternal grandmother, who had died long before. In a sudden rush of wind that sounded the way angel wings might, I felt absolutely enveloped in clear, pure love. And then, layered over these voices and sounds, came another, clearer voice, which seemed to pour right from the heart of God: "See, Anna?" the voice said. "See?"

"See all this beauty, this glory, this goodness," the voice seemed to be telling me. "Here is the heart of the universe. Focus on the good you know exists. Remember this vision of all that is good. You are never alone. You are surrounded by love every step of the way."

I felt less alone on the top of that empty Lindisfarne hill than I had in years. I was absolutely overwhelmed with a sense of the goodness and wholeness of life. I tried to remember and name all the people I cherish, to include them in that moment of pure love. "See, Anna?" God was saying. "See?"

When fear and emptiness threaten me now, I try to slow down and remember the view from that hill. I remind myself that my life, my soul, my heart are not empty. There is no need to fill the vacuum, because no vacuum really exists. God's bottomless well of love sustains me through all my stumbles and peregrinations.

PRAYER SUGGESTION

The Empty Chair

Long ago, a retreat director gave me a xeroxed copy of this great prayer. Anthony de Mello tells the story of a priest who noticed an empty chair at the bedside of a homebound patient he went to visit. The priest asked the patient what the chair was doing there. The patient told him: "I had placed Jesus on that chair and was talking to him when you arrived. . . . For years I found it extremely difficult to pray until a friend explained to me that prayer was a matter of talking to Jesus. He told me to place an empty chair nearby, to imagine Jesus sitting on that chair and to speak with him and to listen to what he says to me in reply. I've had no difficulty praying ever since." Some days later, the story goes, the daughter of the patient came to the rectory to inform the priest that her father had died. She said: "I left him alone for a couple of hours. He seemed so peaceful. When I got back to the room I found him dead. I noticed a strange thing though; his head was resting not on the bed but on a chair that was beside his bed."

This story of the empty chair offers such hope for those times when you don't know what to say to Jesus. All you need to do is place him next to you, in the passenger seat of the car, on the sidewalk as you stroll, on a chair in the kitchen as you prepare dinner. The prayer allows you, just like the second thief, to speak to Jesus right where you are. Just begin talking to him, and see where the conversation leads. Such conversations inevitably will reduce your need to be like a St. Peter's fish. You will be less inclined to fill your empty space with "stuff" as you come to the real understanding that you carry in your spirit your indwelling God.

Afterword

Last winter, my mother had part of her foot amputated as a result of complications from diabetes. She became desolate. After the surgery, she spent months in a rehabilitation center, mired in depression and bowel infections and bedsores. She lost the will to live, even as those around her rallied to her support and implored her to keep trying. The impending birth of her first great-grandchild did nothing to lift her spirits. Sorrow and anger overwhelmed those of us who loved her; sorrow at her suffering, and anger at her refusal to rouse herself. I was helping her eat lunch one day and placed half a turkey sandwich in her hand. She dropped the sandwich onto her hospital bed, saying, "Oh, that sandwich is too heavy."

My mother's decline became an unnameable grief for me, a heaviness that tugged at the very bottom of my heart, weighing down my own spirits. Worry about my mother became my default setting.

One February afternoon, as I tried to work on this book, my mind kept wandering back to the suffering of my family, hampering my ability to write. A friend suggested that I needed a break. He built me a glorious fire and made me a cup of hot chocolate. I settled on the sofa to watch the flames, as a thick, gentle snow blanketed the backyard in a glistening white.

I tried to appreciate the snow and enjoy the fire, but I grew restless and fidgety, staring at the fire with hard eyes and chattering at

God the whole time: "Why is my mother just giving up? How did she get to the point where a turkey sandwich is too much of a burden? How can I help her? How did this situation spin out of control like this?" On and on I raced, frustration whirring in my brain. I must have kept up this one-way diatribe for a full five minutes before I finally asked in exasperation: "God, where are *you* in all of this? Where are you?"

I wasn't expecting a reply.

But from behind my shoulder came four simple words, repeated two times: "I am right here. I am right here." I was so startled that I got up from the sofa and looked out the window into the snow-filled backyard.

I didn't have time to absorb the words before a cardinal appeared, landing on a snow-covered branch. The male cardinal, with his brilliant red plumage, was quickly joined by a female, more muted in color, but still stunning in her contrast with the surrounding whiteness. The sight of the paired birds was heartwarming. Then another cardinal flew onto the evergreen, and another.

"How odd," I thought. "Four cardinals showing up all at once."

The memory of what happened next will stay with me until I face God.

As I stared out the window, mesmerized, cardinal after cardinal filled the trees. They seemed to come from everywhere. I stopped counting after twenty-five. A native midwesterner, I'm accustomed to snowy scenes and landscapes, but I'd never seen such a sight. There in the backyard was a stunning display of red cardinals resting on snow-laden branches. The snow continued to fall as more and more cardinals flew in and out, talking to one another, catching the snowflakes on their bright feathers. The sight made me giddy, and the smile on my face was one of absolute, pure joy. I kept scanning the trees, looking for other types of birds, but only the cardinals were present, with their glossy, vivid plumage sparkling against the snowflakes. I kept expecting the flock of birds to disappear as mysteriously and abruptly as it had appeared. Instead, the visitation of the cardinals endured, and I lingered by the window, unwilling to turn away. In my mind, four simple words animated the view: "I am right here."

In the end, those four words capture what my prayer life has taught me. Nothing I ever do can remove me from the love of God. My existence may temporarily look like a gnarled tangle of black cloth, but God beckons me to keep trying, to keep finding the way to the shining thread in the fabric to become what my Creator calls me to be. I must keep talking to God. Perhaps to human ears, my thoughts and prayers are incoherent. Perhaps in some seasons, all I can muster is a string of anxiety-ridden questions. Maybe, to the outside world, I appear as hopeless as the thief on Calvary. Nonetheless, I know that my transformation in grace depends on my allowing the love of God to work in me and through me: a love that surprises me at every turn; a love that floats on the winds of the North Sea; a love that reminds me, when my path becomes cluttered—"I am right here."

Notes

Chapter 1: The Prayers of Sloppy Sinners

1. Andrew Solomon, *The Noonday Demon: An Atlas of Depression* (New York: Simon and Schuster, 2001), 78.
2. Bruce Feiler, *Walking the Bible* (New York: Perennial, 2002), 117.
3. John Irving, *A Prayer for Owen Meany* (New York: Ballantine, 1989), 310.

Chapter 2: Praying with an Angry Heart

1. W. H. Auden, "Anger," in *The Seven Deadly Sins* (New York: Akadine Press, 2002), 81.
2. Charles Dickens, *David Copperfield* (New York: Signet, 1980), 473
3. David Hassel, S.J., *Radical Prayer* (New York: Paulist Press, 1983), 25–27.

Chapter 3: Praying with a Weary Spirit

1. Evelyn Waugh, "Sloth," in *The Seven Deadly Sins* (New York: Akadine Press, 2002), 58.
2. Ibid., 64.

Chapter 4: Praying with a Lonely Heart

1. Christopher Sykes, "Lust," in *The Seven Deadly Sins* (New York: Akadine Press, 2002), 67.
2. D. H. Lawrence, *Lady Chatterleyís Lover* (New York: Signet, 1962), 134.
3. Saint Patrick's Breastplate prayer is an ancient one and comes to us in many forms. The one printed here follows most closely the version available in Esther de Waal, *The Celtic Way of Prayer* (New York: Image Books, 1999), 18–22.

Chapter 5: Praying with a Prideful Heart

1. John Hardon, *The Catholic Catechism* (New York: Doubleday, 1981), 53.
2. Jane Austen, *Pride and Prejudice* (New York: Norton, 1966), 133.
3. Sally Swift, *Centered Riding* (A Trafalgar Square Farm Book) (North Pomfret, VT: St. Martin's Press, 1985), 10.

Chapter 6: Praying through the Emptiness

1. Patrick Leigh Fermor, "Gluttony," in *The Seven Deadly Sins* (New York: Akadine Press, 2002).
2. John Milton, *Paradise Lost*, Book IX (New York: Odyssey, 1957), 378–405.
3. Ibid.
4. Hubert Van Zeller, *A Book of Beginnings* (Springfield, IL: Templegate Publishers, 1975), 33.